The ~~Ten~~ *Eleven* Commandments of Good Teaching

THIRD EDITION

For teachers everywhere who have devoted themselves to improving the lives of our children. What would we do without you?

The ~~Ten~~ *Eleven* Commandments of Good Teaching

THIRD EDITION

Vickie Gill

CORWIN
A SAGE Company

For information:

Corwin
A SAGE Company
2455 Teller Road
Thousand Oaks,
    California 91320
(800) 233-9936
Fax: (800) 417-2466
www.corwinpress.com

SAGE Pvt. Ltd.
B 1/I 1 Mohan Cooperative
    Industrial Area
Mathura Road, New Delhi 110 044
India

SAGE Ltd.
1 Oliver's Yard
55 City Road
London, EC1Y 1SP
United Kingdom

SAGE Asia-Pacific Pte. Ltd.
33 Pekin Street #02-01
Far East Square
Singapore 048763

Printed in the United States of America

Library of Congress Cataloging-in-Publication Data

Gill, Vickie.
The eleven commandments of good teaching/Vickie Gill. — 3rd ed.
    p. cm.
Includes bibliographical references and index.
ISBN 978-1-4129-7035-8 (cloth)
ISBN 978-1-4129-7036-5 (pbk.)
    1. Effective teaching. I. Title. II. Title: 11 commandments of good teaching.

LB1025.3.G45 2009
371.102—dc22   2009004462

This book is printed on acid-free paper.

09   10   11   12   13   10   9   8   7   6   5   4   3   2   1

Acquisitions Editor:	Jessica Allan
Editorial Assistant:	Joanna Coelho
Production Editor:	Veronica Stapleton
Copy Editor:	Codi Bowman
Typesetter:	C&M Digitals (P) Ltd.
Proofreader:	Dennis W. Webb
Indexer:	Sheila Bodell
Cover Designer:	Rose Storey

Contents

Preface

To be successful, the first thing to do is fall in love with your work.

–Sister Mary Lauretta

In the summer of 1997, I learned that a bright, idealistic young woman had decided that she wasn't cut out to be a teacher because she couldn't get her students to behave. She wasn't in my department and we had rarely spoken, but my heart ached at the thought that a person with such potential would give up after only a year. I decided to sit down and write everything I wish I had said to her in the hopes that she'd give it another try. I organized what I know to be true about good teaching into 10 basic attitudes—commandments, if you will. I wanted to tell her that much of what I know I learned through mistakes, but one of the wonders of our profession is that teachers get a chance to review and renew at the beginning of every year. Sadly, I lost track of her that summer, and I have no idea whether or not she stayed in the profession.

I've been a teacher for 30 years; I love my job, so it upsets me when I see eager, fresh-out-of-college teachers wanting to quit after the first two months. I've spent a great deal of time as a colleague, and now as a mentor, trying to help them find reasons to stay. I know that after the first difficult year, things will get better for them—they just need practical advice from someone who has faced the same challenges.

I have also worked with colleagues who have been in teaching for a long time, but who have lost sight of what attracted them to this job in the first place. Some have become bitter, some have decided to take the path of least resistance, some are just waiting around for retirement. As a kid, I sat through class after class taught by frightened, frustrated newcomers or burned-out lifers. They had lost sight of the joy of teaching, but from their struggles, I created a vision of the teacher that I wanted to become.

In 2000, after a particularly difficult year, I added an eleventh commandment that reminds us that even veterans can feel like novices at times. Eight years later, I've updated the advice in this book to match what I'm currently doing in my classroom. I find that my overall approach to teaching still works; however, I have fine-tuned some of my classroom management techniques and revised teaching units to meet the ever-changing needs of my students, especially with slashed budgets and the dominance of standardized testing in our schools. For this third edition, I've also considered the increasing presence of sophisticated technology in the classroom. We would be foolish to ignore these wonderful tools, but at the same time, the most intuitive Smart Board will never replace knowledgeable, passionate teachers who can inspire their students to master the skills that will be useful both inside and outside of the academic world.

Our students can locate information that will help them pass standardized tests by reading textbooks or searching online—it takes an engaged, inspired teacher to help them believe that these skills are worth mastering. That's what this book is all about—recapturing the passion, figuring out ways to create intimacy in overcrowded classrooms, and making sure that our students feel *seen* and that their teachers are dedicated to their success. It is worthwhile work.

Acknowledgments

I would like to thank the staff at Corwin for their constant support, especially Jessica Allan, Joanna Coelho, and Phyllis Cappello. Thanks also to Gracia Alkema for her confidence in accepting my manuscript for the first edition of this book, and to Rachel Livsey for guiding me through the second edition. As always, this project would not have been completed without the help and encouragement of Kam Jacoby and my daughters, Delaney, Jenny, and Casey. A special thanks to Ken Parker, my new boss, for graciously giving me the time to finish this project—I am inspired by your vision.

In addition, Corwin would like to acknowledge the following peer reviewers for their editorial insight and guidance:

Lisa Garbe
Secondary Literacy Specialist
Tucson Unified School District
Tucson, AZ

Michelle Haj-Broussard
Assistant Professor
McNeese State University
Lake Charles, LA

Dr. Karen Hayes
Associate Professor
Department of Educational Administration and Supervision
University of Nebraska at Omaha

Gayla LeMay
8th Grade History Teacher
Radloff Middle School
Duluth, GA

Alexis Ludewig
2002 Wisconsin Teacher of the Year
Northland Pines School District
Little Chute, WI

Dr. Karen L. Tichy
Associate Superintendent for Instruction
Catholic Education Office, Archdiocese of Saint Louis
Saint Louis, MO

About the Author

 Vickie Gill has taught high school English, reading, and journalism for 30 years in both California and Tennessee. She has a BA in English from San Jose State University and a MEd from Vanderbilt University. Ms. Gill has won several teaching and community service honors and was a finalist for Tennessee State Teacher of the Year in 2000. She is currently teaching part-time and works as a consultant for a school district in Central California. She also maintains a blog about teaching and parenting at http://www.vickiegill.com.

1

Thou Shalt Have a Calling to Teach

Education is what survives when what has been learnt has been forgotten.

—B. F. Skinner

I became a teacher because I detested school—hated just about every minute of it, particularly from sixth grade on. By the time I was in eighth grade, I had a chair of my own right outside the vice-principal's office. I was a teacher's nightmare—the one in the back of the class making noises and comments to make the kids around me laugh. I constantly asked the dreaded question, "Why do we have to learn this stuff anyway?" My teachers would warn me not to get smart with them, which always struck me as a contradiction in terms. I would read every book on the suggested reading lists sent home by my English teachers but refuse to admit that I'd read the books. I didn't want to give my teachers the satisfaction of thinking they had taught me something. I hiked my skirts up, ratted my hair, and sported heavy black eyeliner and white lipstick. When the vice-principal pulled me into her office to wash my face, unroll my skirts, and comb out my hair, I'd march to the closest restroom and redo the whole look. I was one of the girls who wouldn't let you into the bathrooms at lunch because my friends and I were in there smoking.

In my junior year of high school, my counselor called me in to "discuss my future," one of his minimum job requirements. This man had never taken any notice of me before other than to make big circles around my chair outside the vice-principal's door. He sat me in his office, winced as he perused my rather thick disciplinary file, sighed, and asked what I planned to do when I grew up. I smiled and told him I was going to be a teacher. He laughed, looked me dead in the eye, and said, "You'll *never* be a teacher." I got up, leaned over his desk, and said, "You don't know me," and walked out of his office.

> I understood early on that I was not teaching a subject, I was teaching people.

I'd known I was going to be a teacher since I was five years old—it was the only thing I'd ever wanted to do. Even when I was misbehaving in school, causing a couple of teachers to reconsider their chosen profession, I knew teaching was one of the reasons I was put on this earth. Luckily for me, I had parents who never questioned my goals even when I was at my most rebellious. Because I hated to sit still and listen to sermons, I volunteered to work in Sunday school classes from a very early age and discovered I had a knack for working with kids. As I began developing my own ideas about teaching, I was influenced by the failures of the ineffective, joyless teachers I observed as a student. I knew there had to be a better way, so I built my teaching career around engaging the students who hated school the most. In my classes, my students are rewarded for asking, "Why do we have to learn this stuff?" This shows they are concerned with their education.

I understood from the beginning I was not teaching a subject, I was teaching people. I believe my attitude toward school would have been very different if I'd had even one teacher try to figure out why I was acting like such a jerk. I was obviously intelligent, but they settled for stamping all of my report cards with the phrase "not working up to potential." Not one of them ever asked why. If they had, I would have told them I didn't see the usefulness or the excitement in anything they were teaching. It seemed like a complete waste of time to me; one of my teachers even said that high school was a holding zone to keep us teens from glutting the job market. Also, most of my teachers believed students needed to be controlled with a heavy hand; they never understood that true power has more to do with inspiration than intimidation.

I did the bare minimum to graduate from high school and paid for my obstinacy by having to attend a junior college for two years. But college was a revelation for me. The professors didn't care whether I showed up for class or not because I was paying for the privilege. Suddenly, my education became my own. Every class, every credit, was one step closer to my goal, and I blossomed in that atmosphere. Even though it was a painful time for me (and my teachers), my public school experience served me well in that it taught me what not to do as a teacher. For the past 20 years, I've tried to design classes I would like to attend, and it has made all the difference to me and my students.

Sometimes I want to deduct my teaching salary as a charitable contribution on my income-tax forms. It's a huge mistake to get into teaching for the money or because summers are free. Over the years I've known people who became teachers for these reasons, and they spend the money and the summers trying to recover from the physical and psychological stresses the students cause them. I believe you should become a teacher if you would do it anyway, for free. It's one of the hardest jobs I know of, requiring you to act as a gifted academician, psychologist, detective, magician, technician, supervisor, entertainer, and counselor all within a class period—and then do it all over again. My favorite thing about teaching is that it stimulates both my creative and practical impulses. I also love that I am solely responsible for the quality of what goes on in my classroom. As you probably have already surmised, I have some issues with authority figures. However, as a teacher, I am the authority and no one is peering over my shoulder to make sure I'm doing a good job. I am my own quality control, which adds to the pressure and the pleasure of my work.

> *I consider teachers to be among an elite group of people who can truly change the world.*

Teaching is the greatest of all professions. I consider teachers to be among an elite group of people who can truly change the world. I call it the ripple effect. Some time ago, I was talking with a group of people who were in college in the early 1970s, a time of tremendous social upheaval and change. We were laughing about the protest marches, the campus takeovers, and the hubristic attitude that made us believe that if we handed out enough leaflets the world would slap its collective forehead and shout, "Of course you're right—why didn't I think of peace and love and feeding the children!" Instead, even after toppling an administration, it was business as usual. One person in the group shook his head at what naive fools we'd been, noting that not one of us had followed an idealistic path. I told him that I had—I became a teacher. Instead of trying to change thousands of minds at once, I influence people daily in a much smaller arena. It is possible that my students will raise their children with enlightened attitudes about racism, sexism, and their responsibilities to their communities. It's like dropping a pebble in a pool—I can't change everything, but I can help my students to examine why they believe what they do and to live a more deliberate life.

You're a closely watched role model who communicates more by what you do than by what you say.

If teaching were easy, anyone could do it. Teachers bear an overwhelming responsibility because a teacher's casual comment can become part of a student's life script. How many times have you heard adults say that a teacher's encouragement influenced them to change the course of their lives? On the other hand, I know several adults who speak bitterly of teachers who told them in third grade they were insipid, untalented, or a waste of time; these adults have never forgotten those words. As a teacher, you're not allowed to have such a bad day that you take it out on your students. As a teacher, you're a closely watched role model who communicates more by what you do than by what you say. As a teacher, you are remembered forever, but *how* you are remembered is up to you. Teaching is an incredibly important and demanding job, and it requires a profound commitment. The first commandment of good teaching? Thou shalt not become a teacher unless you feel a calling to this wellspring of all professions. Depending on your talent and disposition, teaching can be the best or the worst way to earn your living.

2

Thou Shalt Demonstrate and Project the Joy of Learning

If you want to build a ship, don't drum up people together to collect wood and don't assign them tasks and work, but rather teach them to long for the endless immensity of the sea.

—Antoine de Saint-Exupéry

When I lived in Tennessee, I was married to a songwriter, so I often attended parties or showcases with people who were not in the field of education. For a long time, I dreaded the moment when someone would ask what I did for a living because the minute I said I was a teacher people's attitudes changed. Either their eyes glazed over and they suddenly noticed a long-lost friend across the room or they straightened up, shifted uncomfortably, and hid their cigarettes behind their backs. If I foolishly added I was an English teacher, all conversation sputtered to a painful end. I realized that the general

7

population's impression is that many teachers are judgmental, anal-retentive control freaks who somehow could deduct points at a party for poor grammar. Some people I met continued talking to me, complimenting me on sacrificing my life to such a thankless job. It became so annoying that I developed my own defense mechanisms. Sometimes I made a joke and said, "Excuse me, I do believe you've misplaced your modifier." Other times, I thanked the person for reducing me to a stereotype and moved on. But the easiest response was to sidestep the question and avoid mentioning teaching at all. What's wrong with this picture? I honestly love my job and am tremendously proud of what I do.

Why do people have the impression that teaching is a boring, joyless profession? Maybe it's because they've all been in boring, joyless classes. I have three daughters who spent 12 years in the public school system. I watched them evolve from ravenous learners to bored participants, fulfilling the minimum requirements to maintain their class rankings. When they were little, they were interested in everything—learning was not compartmentalized, labeled, or evaluated. They did it naturally. When they entered school, they quickly realized that going along with the program was the easiest way to survive. In most of their classes, they were placed in desks in rows, handed worksheets, and rewarded for not asking why this was happening. Their main goal was to move through the system as quickly as possible so they could get on with "real life." My daughters were very bright children with a great deal of self-control; imagine how painful school is for kids with learning disabilities or behavior problems.

> *Why do people have the impression that teaching is a boring, joyless profession? Maybe it's because they've all been in boring, joyless classes.*

But along the way, my girls had a few remarkable teachers who stood out like beacons in a dense fog. What was different about these people? I believe these teachers clearly demonstrated and projected the joy of learning. Their classes were designed for success, accommodated differences, and gave the impression that magic might break out at any moment. These teachers obviously loved students, viewed them as individuals, and delighted in their uniqueness. These teachers never stopped learning themselves and shared with their students some new discovery or insight that had intrigued or charmed them. These teachers made learning so exciting the students didn't want to stay home for fear of missing something really great. These teachers loved what they did, and the students knew it.

Take time to remember what drew you to teaching in the first place. What kinds of things did your favorite teachers do?

I think that one of the great burdens of being a teacher is that we are constant role models. The students watch everything we do, which can be exhausting. Teaching has a great deal in common with acting and sales. Not only do we need to be completely knowledgeable about the subjects we teach, we also have to make the students want to buy what we're offering. One of the biggest arguments I have ever had with a colleague was whether teachers needed to motivate students. My colleague felt students should come to him predisposed to learn—that was their job. His job was to disseminate the information. I told him the administration would be happy to hear about his attitude. If all this teacher needed to do was disseminate information, we could pass out textbooks, slide a recording of him at his best into the VCR, and fire his sorry self, thus saving the school system thousands of dollars over the years.

One of the most useful things you can do as a teacher is take time to remember what drew you to teaching in the first place. What kinds of things did your favorite teachers do? What made you fall in love with the subject you teach? What was the atmosphere and layout of your favorite class? Which lessons made an impression on you? What was useful later in your life? One of my personal goals is that the students will leave my room at the end of the year with a clear understanding of why I save time out of every day to read for pleasure and why I believe writing to be an invaluable tool for solving problems and creating opportunities.

Another advantage for any teacher is the ability to remember what it's like to be a kid. A few years ago, I attended an inservice workshop with about 50 other teachers from my school district. The presenter asked the teachers to think back to their two most significant memories of high school. He then asked how many of these memories happened inside the classroom. Not one hand was raised. Many of us noted that what really mattered to us in school were sports, social events, broken hearts, cliques, fights, and awards. Most of what we learned academically had long been forgotten unless it was related to the subject we were currently teaching. Another of my goals is that students will talk about something they learned in my class long after they exit the education system.

> *A sign in my classroom says, "Education is either to calm the disturbed or disturb the calm."*

I have a sign in my classroom that says, "Education is either to calm the disturbed or disturb the calm." This has profoundly affected the way I teach. I discuss this saying with my classes on the first day of school, asking them whether they classify themselves as among the calm or among the disturbed. This usually creates a lively discussion, and I get immediate insights into some of my students. I point out that many of them have drifted through school for years, sitting quietly, doing whatever was required, questioning nothing, and waiting for the bell to ring. These are the "calm," and my job is to disturb them. I need to convince them to take charge of their own education, analyzing information rather than just regurgitating it. I work with them in small groups so that they cannot hide in the back of the class; each of them has to be prepared to defend an answer. I let them know that in my class there is a great tolerance for differences of opinion, but everyone must have an opinion and be able to back it up. Then, I address the "disturbed." These are the students who have what I call noisy minds. Perhaps their personal lives are in such chaos that they feel the school has nothing to offer of any use. Others are extremely bright students who have become openly hostile to the mediocrity of most class work. My job is to show them how the skills I'm teaching can help them take control of their lives and futures. My job is to make them think something they have never thought before. My job is to help them turn down the noise in their minds so they can concentrate on the academic skills that will make them successful.

> My students are stunned when I tell them that if I were a millionaire, I would teach for free. I'd just start a little later in the day and skip the paperwork.

Passionate teachers should thank the few really terrible teachers in their schools because they make our work much easier. Poor teachers spend so much time boring, humiliating, or trying to control students that when the kids come to a dynamic classroom, it's like a breath of fresh air. Our classes should be safe, exciting, authentic learning environments where mistakes and disabilities are just useful information. My students are stunned when I tell them that if I were a millionaire, I would teach for free. I'd just start a little later in the day and skip the paperwork. I want to be one of the few adults they know who loves her work. I use this fact as a launching pad for a unit on their goals. I try to help them focus on their calling—on what gives them joy—and determine how to make a living doing it.

Every year I have several students who laugh when I tell them money should not be a deciding factor in choosing a career. Some are quite straightforward in pointing out what a sucker I am to settle for a teacher's pay. Last year, one senior told me that if it paid enough, he'd be willing to do anything. I suggested that if he were offered one job doing something he loved for $15 an hour and another job doing something he hated for $30 an hour, he'd be a fool to take the higher-paying job. He laughed and said that if the pay was good, he didn't care what he was required to do.

It took only a few minutes to change his mind. I asked him to think about the class in school he had hated the most—the one he thought he'd never get through because it was so boring and the teacher was so awful. Then I told him I'd pay him $30 an hour to sit in that class all day every day for the next 25 years. That got his attention. How could a person who became a teacher because of the love of a subject or a desire to help young people design a class so abhorrent that this student would cut his salary in half for the rest of his life to avoid it?

Human beings are born to learn. Babies do it so naturally it's almost impossible to keep them from it. Ask kindergartners about their future plans and they shout out an eclectic set of goals involving careers as singers-doctors-astronauts-veterinarians-preachers-mommies all at the same time. Ask a group of high school students what they want to do for a living and it's likely the majority of them will shrug their shoulders and mutter, "I don't know." What happened in those 12 years?

The second commandment of good teaching? Thou shalt demonstrate and project the joy of learning.

3

Thou Shalt Keep Your Eyes on the Prize

They know enough who know how to learn.

—Henry Adams

Now that you have a vision of teaching at its best, how do you develop a curriculum that nurtures that vision? How do you choose what to teach? In a course I took in graduate school, the instructor asked, "What's worth knowing?" The class was full of teachers working on master's degrees, and I could tell many of them felt this was a pointless question. But I found it exhilarating. It really drove me to examine what I was teaching. Earlier, I mentioned getting into trouble as a kid for asking why we had to learn what the teacher was presenting. To me, that should be the most significant question the teacher addresses. If you plan to design your class around your state's prepared curriculum, be sure you have an answer to that question. And in my opinion, the following answers are not okay:

- Your teacher next year will expect you to know this.
- Because I told you so.
- You'll be asked this material on a test.
- This is what every class at this level is studying.
- It's none of your business.
- If I had to suffer through this so should you.

Recently, I asked four honor students who excelled in advanced math how they might use what they'd learned. The best answer was they may need it later in life or it was good exercise for the brain. Not one of them could tell me how they could use the math they had learned even though they were glad they'd taken the classes. I think the reason so little of what students study in school stays with them is because no one has demonstrated the usefulness of the information. One of my brothers uses geometry and algebra to design decks, but he admits when he was learning those skills in high school, he had no idea they could be applied to construction. In my experience, I never really learned anything until I had to use it. Good teachers provide practical applications for the facts they're presenting so they prepare their students to be more than great Trivial Pursuit players.

> *I never really learned anything until I had to use it. Good teachers provide practical applications for the facts they're presenting.*

Whenever I design a curriculum, I always ask myself what I want the students to be able to do when they leave the class. In other words, I start from the big picture and then work backward. This idea has been around for a long time, but it's enjoying a resurgence in teacher training courses. In their book *Understanding by Design*, Grant Wiggins and Jay McTighe (2005) refer to this as *backward design* and encourage teachers to begin with *essential questions*. These are the ones I posed for my students at the beginning of this school year:

What and why should I read?

How do I make my writing worth reading?

What do I need to memorize?

How do I locate what I need to know?

What are the beliefs on which I base my life?

Why was I put on this Earth and what am I going to do about it?

I also ask my students on the first day of class, "What are the characteristics of an educated person?" We toss around ideas for a while, and I write all their responses on the board. Usually, they include items such as having a big vocabulary or quoting Shakespeare as signs of an educated person. I always ask if the ability to fix a car engine or design a house might label a person as educated. After much discussion, I try to lead them to consider the following attributes:

- Educated people can find out what they need to know.
- Educated people share a common body of knowledge with other educated people that aids them in finding out what they need to know.
- Educated people are curious; they are lifelong learners.

In simplified forms, these are my three main teaching goals. Of course, in reality these goals are huge, especially when students enter my class completely uninterested in finding out anything, with an uncommonly small body of knowledge, and with their minds tightly shut. But it's a starting place.

What are the characteristics of an educated person?

Another sign in my room says, "If you find what is within you, what you find will save you; if you do not find what is within you, what you do not find will destroy you." Many of the lessons I teach are designed to help students discover what they are meant to do. I know this sounds beyond the realm of what schools should be required to do, but until students focus on some personal goals, most of what they learn in your class will be forgotten after the final exam.

The only adults in the world who are ever asked to identify nouns and verbs are English teachers.

I'm blessed because I teach English—in my mind, the greatest of all subjects because it involves reading, writing, and thinking. These three skills are so flexible that I can create a curriculum to address almost any need my students may have. For example, I begin every semester with a unit on personal goals. This unit enables me to pretest my students' writing skills by having them describe their plans for the next 10 years. The result is a fairly accurate picture of the students' writing abilities and the kind of remediation they need to reach their goals. It also sets up a discussion topic of high interest for the first small-group meetings. The students who are already focused can share their plans, and the clueless can start considering some options. During this unit, the students complete an online questionnaire that suggests possible careers based on their responses to questions about their interests, skills, and plans. This program also gives up-to-date information about job requirements, salaries, training, and availability. It includes a database of colleges throughout the state and information about getting into those colleges. We do all sorts of personality and interest analysis exercises, constantly trying to match each student to a career. I make up several large posters that display students with common career goals, and these are posted in the front of the room. The students eventually write letters to colleges researching financial aid and admission requirements. We have speakers from various businesses drop in to tell students about their jobs and, more important, about what they expect from employees.

Please note that no busywork is assigned during this unit. The usefulness of everything they do is obvious to the students as they discover the power of the written word through writing letters and the advantage of being able to read quickly as they seek information that will help them tackle the puzzle of their futures.

Midway through the career unit, I give the students a long-term assignment to locate someone working in a field in which they are interested. They are to contact this person and ask for a sample of on-the-job writing he or she does as a regular part of the job. Every year I have one or two students who swear that their future career involves no writing whatsoever— some recent searches included ski patrol, paintball event coordinator, and professional baseball player. Through various means, we were able to locate someone currently employed in each of these careers, and in each case, the person was more than happy to share the type of writing that was required. The students were shocked but thrilled when they received copies of rescue reports, flyers for paintball contests, and speeches given to community groups.

I know most of the curriculum frameworks you receive from state departments of education start with big goals that are then broken down into objectives. But quite often, teachers focus so much on moving through the objectives that they lose sight of the big picture. When I began teaching in Tennessee, a colleague and I disagreed over what should be taught in a high school English class. She insisted I should work from the state-adopted grammar and literature textbooks, moving through the objectives in exactly the same time frame as other English teachers. I pointed out that it was not unusual for me to have students in my senior English class who had done precious little writing because of this inflexible focus on the parts rather than the whole. She countered that the students had to master basic grammatical skills before they could possibly hope to write a composition. I asked her how she thought a baby should be taught to walk. Should we put the child in a high chair and show him diagrams of the leg, requiring him to memorize the names of all of the moving parts? Should we show films to the baby of people walking? Or should we put the baby on the floor and let him stumble and fall again and again until one day the baby stays up? This is exactly what we do when we teach writing.

In terms of the big picture, the only adults in the world who are ever asked to identify nouns and verbs are English teachers. Everyone else just unconsciously uses these parts of speech. Students need to write and write and write some more. They need to write letters that are really mailed and compositions that analyze their opinions. They need to read articles about marriage and parenting and write responses describing what they will do in these relationships. These topics and projects are not only of special interest to teenagers, they are essential to the students' futures. I further annoyed my colleague during our conversation by pointing out that if I ever needed to take a year off from teaching for whatever reason, I'd just pass out the grammar books, give a 15-minute lecture on nouns and verbs, and then have the students do problems 1 to 50 at the end of the chapter while I kick back at my desk. There is so little time and so much to do in a class period; we must focus on the most effective methods available. If a student has been using grammar and spelling texts for nine years and still doesn't get it, then this is an ineffectual use of time, and we should try something else.

> *Choosing goals on the first day of a semester forces the students to take responsibility for what will go on in my class.*

I need to tell you at this point that I do teach to tests. My students will not graduate from high school unless they pass the state competency test, and they will limit their college choices unless they score reasonably well on the SAT or ACT. I understand this, but I have to make this their choice. On the first day of the semester, I pass out a worksheet with a long list of goals—things I can teach relating to reading, writing, and thinking. One of the goals is to pass the state exit exam or prepare for high-stakes standardized tests. I then ask the students to place a checkmark next to all of the things they'd like to tackle during the semester. Finally, I ask them to circle the three goals of most importance to them. Quite often, high-school students will highlight preparing for the SAT as a real concern.

I believe this activity accomplishes two things. One, it tells me what my students think they need to know. I can then group students with common goals. Two, it forces the students to take responsibility for what happens in my class. It gives them a sense of ownership and that they are not simply empty vessels into which I will pour what I think they need. When I surprise the students with a timed, in-class essay with an SAT-style prompt, they recognize it as a stressful but necessary activity that they themselves requested.

You would be amazed at how this worksheet increases the students' focus—and their discomfort. Some of the students don't want to admit they are in school to learn anything at all. They see school as a holding zone, keeping them from enjoying real life. A while back, I passed out the goal sheets to a group of 9th-, 10th-, and 11th-grade students in my reading lab. When I collected the sheets, one boy handed me a blank sheet of paper, with nothing but his name on top. He looked at me defiantly, hoping for his first skirmish to establish the battle lines. Instead, I glanced at the paper, gazed at him fondly, and murmured, "This is wonderful." He shifted uncomfortably and said, "What do you mean?" I smiled and answered that by not checking anything, he was telling me he wanted to learn everything, and he was my favorite kind of student. I told him I appreciated his confidence in me and that I'd do everything I could to help him succeed. He eyed me suspiciously for a while, but he was onboard for the rest of the year.

This is why the first week of school is so hectic. I have to find out what my students need before I can create the objectives.

In my experience, preparing for state competency tests is rather boring for both teachers and students. However, when it's the students' choice, it adds new energy and dedication to the pursuit of this goal. Because the test takes place about six weeks after the semester begins, I make this an intensive, all-out attack, with the promise of much more interesting reading, writing, and thinking activities after the test is over. Imagine—reading, writing, and thinking are the rewards the students look forward to.

A few years ago, one of my supervisors asked to see the objectives for my reading lab for the upcoming school year. He called me at home in July and said he needed to see what I would be teaching for a state department form he was completing. I told him I could not possibly know my objectives until I met my students. This just stunned him, and he accused me of teaching without a plan. I told him I could easily hand him a beautifully sequenced set of objectives lifted straight from the state's curriculum guide for the basic competency test—this would be no problem. But what if, when I met my students in the fall, 90% of them had passed the competency test? What if some couldn't read at all? What if some were fairly good readers, but they struggled with writing? What if some had such severe emotional problems that they couldn't concentrate? I explained to my supervisor this is why the first week of school is so hectic—I have to find out what my students need before I can create the objectives. However, I did add that my main goal was to turn out educated people, told him the three characteristics of an educated person, and suggested he write that on his form.

When deciding what to teach, you have to trust your instincts. I can picture several of my former supervisors shifting uneasily in their chairs thinking of those incompetent teachers who show movies all day or let the students sit and talk as long as they leave the teacher alone. My response is that these people are not teachers and should not be in the profession. If someone so incompetent has been hired and has maintained his or her job through tenure, then it's the principal's problem to ensure that at least the state's guidelines are followed. But it is not the principal's job to tamper with authentic teaching that works. Figure out what you want your students to be able to do when they leave your class, make sure these objectives match what they need to be successful in life, and pass on the joy of learning that made you choose your subject in the first place. Be original and teach in the style that works best for you. The third commandment of good teaching? Thou shalt know where you are going and keep your eyes on the prize.

4

Thou Shalt Be Organized and Accountable

I am a craftsperson with young people to the point where it is both free and structured, spontaneous and disciplined, innovative and classical, fun and very difficult.

—Herbert Kohl

Most people who are good at what they do work really hard, and what I'm about to suggest in this chapter will definitely present a challenge to you. Now that you've captured the vision of what you want to teach—the big picture—the next task is to brainstorm all of the steps that take the students to those goals. After that, you need to identify the best ideas, sequence them into teaching units, and then plan activities that demonstrate and promote the skills the students will need to reach the original goals.

When brainstorming, allow yourself to be completely nonjudgmental—no idea is too silly or too difficult. Leave yourself open to everything. Some of my best teaching ideas come from the oddest places. I constantly rip quotes, addresses, or articles out of magazines and newspapers. I subscribe to English journals, magazines, and newspapers. I record much of what I watch on TV so I can stop the program and write down a quote or an idea. I participate in an Internet discussion group about the teaching of reading and writing. I constantly ask people I meet from all walks of life to identify the most useful things they learned in school. I interview employers and personnel directors to find out what they want us to teach in the schools. At the end of most school years, I tell people who ask about my job that I just had my best teaching experience ever. And by September, I'm trying something new.

One of the major goals I have for my English students is for them to write a college-level research paper in Modern Language Association (MLA) format. To prepare the students for this project, I introduce them to the techniques of research through a unit on debate. Their first assignment is to outline and write a four-paragraph paper presenting both sides of a controversial issue. Through this assignment, I can show them how to write an introduction, conclusion, and supporting points, and how to separate themselves from a topic. I tell the students that they can never really win a debate until they thoroughly understand the beliefs of the opposition. I point out this skill will serve them well in their relationships at home and on the job. Summarizing the opinions of people whose beliefs are the antithesis of their own is a difficult assignment for some students but an enlightening experience.

Meanwhile, I prepare them for an actual debate. The class votes on two or three controversial issues, and I let them select the topic of their choice. The only catch is that they don't know which side of the issue they will be defending until the day before the debate. At this point, the assignment really gets interesting and authentic learning occurs. Often, students are highly opinionated about a number of topics, but they haven't a clue as to what the opposition will say. Sometimes during this activity, I can literally see their minds open.

A number of years ago, one of my students in senior English was the most overtly racist person I had ever met. His racism ran so deep that when he said highly offensive things in class, he didn't have that look of defiance sported by most people trying to shock others; this was his family's truth. He and I had already exchanged some heated sentiments about this during the semester, and he knew I would not tolerate these comments in my classroom. At the time, the news was filled with stories about a proposal to remove images of the Confederate flag from public buildings in the South because many viewed it as a racist symbol. Joe had voiced his opinion about this a number of times during the semester, claiming it was his right as a Southerner to display this sign of pride in his heritage. His great-great-granddaddy had fought for the South in the Civil War, and he had gone so far as to have the flag tattooed on his chest and painted on the roof of his truck. He would not listen to other points of view and said that anyone who didn't like it could go live with the Yankees. When it came time to choose debate topics, he raised his hand, smirked at his buddies, and suggested that we should make it a law that the Confederate flag must be flown in front of every school and courthouse in the South. He expected me to comment on his suggestion, but I never missed a beat and wrote his topic on the board with the others.

He generated enough support in the class to have his proposal voted as one of the three to be argued the following week. Two days before the debate, the eight students who signed up for the Confederate flag issue gathered before me to draw "for" and "against" slips from a basket on my desk. As luck would have it, Joe drew an "against" paper. He was furious, but I told him that I had honored his input and now it was his turn to honor the rules of the debate. Most of his friends predicted that he would skip school that day, but he was there, he was prepared, and he dazzled the audience by pointing out that the flag represented the proslavery forces in the Civil War and has been adopted by such groups as the Ku Klux Klan. He argued passionately and intelligently for racial harmony. When the opposing team tried to use his tattoo against him, he startled us all by unbuttoning his shirt to reveal a large Band-Aid on his chest. He claimed that he had his tattoo removed the day before when he realized how painful a symbol it was for those whose ancestors had been slaves. I about fell out of my chair laughing, and despite the theatrics, the audience chose his team as the winners of the debate. Afterward, he made sure everyone knew his tattoo was intact and that he had only said those things for a grade. But I knew he had at least considered both sides of an opinion he'd never questioned. I have no idea if he ever softened his racist views or changed his actions in any way, but I was extremely proud of him for those 15 minutes, and I knew he would not soon forget the experience.

> *I believe that for every objective you choose to teach, you can design meaningful, exciting, and authentic activities to reach your goal.*

This debate unit takes about two weeks of the semester, but as you can see, a myriad of valuable skills are practiced in a dynamic atmosphere designed to engage every student. Most of the employers I talk with want us to teach basic reading, writing, math, computer, communication, and teamwork skills. When the students include statistics in their arguments, this unit does it all. I believe that for every objective you choose to teach, you can design meaningful, exciting, and authentic activities to reach your goal. In my reading lab, I work with many students who are reading anywhere from 2 to 10 years below their grade level. Some of these students are parents, and a few are even married. Because most have some sort of learning disability, it is very likely they will pass this struggle with the printed word on to their children. So in the course of teaching them to read, I also teach them how to teach someone else to read. For example, I have some students who need to review basic phonetic principles, such as short vowel sounds, and this can be humiliating for a 16-year-old. When I begin the class, I tell my students that at the end of the semester we will be going to a primary school three times a week to tutor little kindergarten through second-grade students. Therefore, they need to pay close attention to everything I show them because they will be assigned a student of their own to teach. This really gets their attention. As I work with the group studying vowel sounds, I also demonstrate to them how to teach their own children to read. After years of working with this cross-age tutoring program, I'm not convinced my students dramatically raise the reading levels of the primary-school children. But I do know these experiences have raised my students' reading levels and have provided a healthy boost to their self-esteem.

This brings us to one of the most important characteristics of good teaching: you must develop a system to document what you do. Every year, I work with students who have received passing grades in all of their English classes as well as on the state competency test. The only problem is that they can barely read and write. I don't believe a list of grades is a useful indicator of a student's progress. As a supplement, I keep a portfolio for each of my students. I know this sounds like just more paperwork, but it's the most accurate way I can demonstrate what a student has accomplished in my class. For example, the portfolios of my senior English students contain a set of pretests (writing, reading comprehension, spelling, listening skills, goals, and so on) and several assignments done in class on the computer that are relatively error-free, including a cover letter and résumé, as well as several typed essays. At the end of the semester, I give each student a large envelope containing examples of their early work and their perfect papers, including three copies of their résumés and their corrected research paper. I tell them to put this envelope in their underwear drawers for safekeeping because every paper will be useful to them later in college or when they look for a job. This is amazing to most of them. They often comment that this was the first class in which they could clearly see what they had accomplished and the first class in 12 years that required them to do something again and again until it was perfect.

So how do you keep up with the constant correcting and monitoring that this system requires? My solution is to work with my students in three small groups. The maximum number of students in my reading lab is 15 per class, and I've convinced my administrators to put no more than 30 students in my English classes. My school has adopted the four-period-day schedule, requiring me to teach three classes a day. Each class period is 90 minutes, so I meet with each small group for about 25 minutes per class period. As I'm meeting with one group, the second group is working on the computers, using writing, spelling, vocabulary, or career programs. The students in the third group are in their seats working on the assignment they will bring to me to discuss or correct in a few minutes.

> *I'm aware that for many of my students, I'm one of the few adults with whom they have a meaningful conversation all day.*

This system accomplishes a number of things. First, it creates a businesslike atmosphere in the classroom—everyone is engaged all of the time, and a cardinal rule is that the class must be quiet enough so the group working with me is not disturbed. I often tell the students, "If I'm working, you're working," and they see me teach all period. Second, the small groups create informal settings in which the 10 students can take risks and get individual attention from me. Third, I can assign a great deal of writing because I quickly rotate each student to the chair on either side of me to review the assignment immediately. When teaching grammar and usage, I assign three to five sentence summaries of articles or short stories. These are typed and double-spaced so that the errors they leave on the page are concepts the students truly don't understand. I can read each student's work rather quickly and offer individualized minilessons on grammar and structure. I used to take home stacks of essays, correct them over a day or two, and then hand them back covered with red ink, proving only that I am a good proofreader. Reviewing the work shortly after it's written gives the student immediate feedback; also, because I'll be sitting right next to them when I go over their work, it encourages the students to look it over carefully before they print. Fourth, meeting in small groups is a great way for me to get to know my students as individuals. A student can't remain invisible in my class; I counted on that sense of anonymity when I was a teenager because I didn't want to feel a sense of responsibility for the teacher's feelings. I'm aware that for many of my students, I'm one of the few adults with whom they have a meaningful conversation all day. Finally, my system largely eliminates certain "techniques" many students have mastered by high school: copying someone else's homework and uncanny peripheral vision. I rarely assign worksheets or questions from the textbook, so I can quickly tell when someone is trying to pass off another student's work as his or her own.

A few years ago, I worked with a difficult young man who had become very good at passing classes by forcing other students to share homework or test answers. It took some time for me to convince him that (a) I read every piece my students write, sometimes several times, and (b) I'm not an idiot. I knew he'd been goofing off on the computers, but when his group came to the board, he turned in a beautiful, one-page, double-spaced composition about his career goals. He'd accessed another student's file, deleted her name, and added his own. Evidently, several of his previous teachers had graded papers by weighing or measuring, and he'd been rewarded with passing grades. As I glanced over the paper, I immediately remembered where I had seen it before, so I found the girl's portfolio and pulled both the students into the hallway. I gave the girl a wink as I pretended to lambaste her for turning in plagiarized work. I purposely didn't look directly at the boy, but I could see his face getting redder and redder as the girl protested her innocence. Finally, he admitted copying her paper, and I advised him to read enough next time to at least know that his conclusion proudly announced his plans to become a mother before starting his career.

To use this small-group system of managing classes, you have to be extremely organized, but also flexible. My daily lesson plans are written in pencil in case they need to be revised, or I'll use sticky notes if I need to move activities to the next day. I've designed a chart showing me at a glance what each group should be doing during the 25-minute sessions. The seat assignments are written on a whiteboard at the back of the class, and the necessary materials are laid out before the day begins. I train the students to glance at the front board when they walk into class to see where their group should be when class begins. When I'm introducing a new unit or novel, I'll write "all together" on the front board, and the kids know to get ready to take notes and participate in class discussions. Especially for English teachers, it's important to pace the written assignments so you don't have to stay after school or work on weekends just to keep up with grading. Larger essays and research papers need to be evaluated outside of class, but by working with the kids in groups, much of the grading can be done as soon as they finish. In many ways, that's the most teachable time, and the students take the work home for revision. It's important to have the students staple the revised writing to the original and place it in their portfolios so you can trace their progress over the school year.

> *There is always something for the students to do, and they get individualized attention.*

Because I work with the students for only 25 minutes per group, it's very important that I have the full time with them. This system eliminates many behavior problems because there is always something for the students to do, and they get individualized attention, which increases their chances for success. To give the kids my complete focus, I assign a contact person for each group. I do this at the end of the first week of class because by then it's fairly obvious which students know something about computers, have reasonable social skills, and can follow instructions. Students who have trouble on the computers or with the seatwork know to quietly ask their contact person before asking me. A majority of the problems can be handled this way, allowing me to work with my small group undisturbed.

Besides the test, quiz, and homework grades, I also put a participation/effort grade in my grade book every two weeks. This is determined by a daily chart I keep indicating how students worked during the class period. Each day when the students leave, I quickly mark a plus, a check, or a minus next to their names. A plus means they worked all period and were prepared when they came to the small group to work with me. A check means I had to speak to them to remind them to get to work or they caused a slight disturbance in the class but got right back to work. A minus means they had a bad day, getting little done, trying to sleep, or causing such a disturbance I had to divert my attention from the small group to deal with their problems. These marks break down into numerical values: A plus equals 10 points, a check 5 points, and a minus 0 points, with a possible perfect score of 100. This grade rewards the students in the class who have poor English skills and really struggle with their assignments and tests but work hard every day to improve. It also challenges students who come to the class with excellent English skills but are used to doing only what is necessary to get by. These students can ace a test but waste a tremendous amount of time, usually disturbing other people while they do it. Also, these students will make the worst kinds of employees unless they learn that they will be paid based on their efforts and that their job is to be productive. Sometimes the kids beg for a free day or a movie or something. I tell them they've already mastered movie viewing, sitting around talking, and sleeping. In fact, most of them could earn a PhD in those areas. I point out it would be wrong of me to allow them to practice skills they've already mastered; this would be an insult to their intelligence.

Teaching can eat up your life—it is very possible to spend all day and night in your school trying to help everyone and keeping up with your work.

Getting organized pays off for you in a number of ways. Your students will have confidence in what you're teaching because you have an agenda and know specifically where you're going. There is always something meaningful to do if you have to substitute one activity for another. You eliminate a large portion of discipline problems because you don't spend the first part of each class scrambling to find materials that you forgot to prepare. Also, if parents or administrators have questions about a student's grades or work, you have the documentation at your fingertips. Finally, you put in less overtime because you've developed a system that works within the given time constraints. Remember that teaching can eat up your life—it is very possible to spend all day and night in your school trying to help everyone and keeping up with your work. You can never give enough. As passionate as I am about my job, I have a life away from the classroom that is equally important and needs to be protected. This life not only shields me from burnout, it also makes me a more interesting, well-rounded role model for my students. The fourth commandment of good teaching? Thou shalt be organized and accountable for your students' success.

5

Thou Shalt Ask and Ye May Receive

The best way to predict your future is to create it.

—Abraham Lincoln

U p to this point, I've tried to describe teaching as a visionary's job that can wear you out. You may be ready to shout, "Check, please!" and look for employment in the recreation-and-leisure field. But there are ways to make your life as a teacher much easier. The most useful method is to figure out specifically the tools you need to do the best job you can and then ask for them. The worst thing that can happen is someone says no and you have to look elsewhere or modify your plans. But it's been my experience that people say yes more often than no and that those who get are those who ask.

Quite often a colleague will come into my classroom to borrow something or to ask my advice. This is usually a teacher who is struggling with his or her students. During the course of our conversation, this person often says, "Well, I'd have it made, too, if I had this big room and all of these computers." Sometimes the comment is designed to make me feel guilty for my wealth, but it doesn't work. I have a bank of computers, along with printers, scanners, and such because I asked for them. That person didn't. I'm not so naive as to think that all my colleagues need to do is run to the front office and hand the principal a list of items they want for their classrooms. This probably won't work, although I've gotten a number of things I've needed by describing to my principal the really cool project I'm working on that would bring glory and honor to our school, if I only had a certain piece of equipment or if he'd pay to send me to a conference somewhere. I've been taken aback a number of times by how easily the principal has agreed. I admit that it is a good idea to keep an ear to the ground about what's going on elsewhere in the school, and the bookkeeper or secretaries can be incredibly helpful in choosing the right moment to approach the administrator. It also helps if you have proved to be an effective and useful teacher. The point is that you'll never get what you need unless you ask. "No" is not a rejection, just a detour.

> *It is a good idea to keep an ear to the ground about what's going on elsewhere in the school.*

When I was designing my class, I knew I needed to have enough computers so that I could work with the students in small groups. I had a few computers that my brother, who worked for IBM, had helped me acquire, but they were discontinued models and woefully out-of-date. One day I was in a teachers' meeting and the principal was describing a new system the counselors would be using to help students plan for their futures. All eighth graders would be required to choose either a college-prep or a tech-prep track when choosing classes to take in high school. The goal was to raise the requirements for graduation and eliminate the situation where a student is handed a diploma but is prepared for neither college nor work. The state department of education had mandated that the schools raise the requirements and quality of all high-school classes to avoid the embarrassment of graduates who couldn't read their diplomas.

This great idea gave me a great idea. I wrote a proposal for a reading and writing lab designed to help students increase their skills to the point where they could succeed in these more challenging classes. When I presented my proposal to the school board, I emphasized that it would be imprudent to require more from the students without offering support classes to get them up to par. Therefore, I was offering my services as the coordinator of this new reading lab to help ensure a quality education for all graduates. All I needed to accomplish this were some up-to-date computers. The board promised to get back to me, and I held my breath. A few weeks later, the technology coordinator called to say the board had approved my plan, and the superintendent wanted to know how many computers I needed. I'd been around the block with this sort of thing before, so I asked for twice as many as I wanted. "Ten," I said. She said, "Okay, anything else?" I almost fainted but recovered quickly. "And a couple of printers!" "Okay, anything else?" Now I was scrambling. "And educational software and printer paper!" She told me she'd get the order right out and the equipment would be delivered to my classroom by the beginning of the school year. I was stunned. They were giving me far more than I expected just because I asked.

> *I was stunned. They were giving me far more than I expected just because I asked.*

Later, when I was assigned to teach a journalism class, I was able to get a phone in my classroom. In my rural Tennessee high school, few teachers had phones in their rooms, and this had always been a real inconvenience. However, in 1995, it was considered too much an expense to be justified. I told my principal that my journalism students needed to sell ads and interview people in the community as part of their class work and a phone was essential for a class such as this. I also pointed out that the yearbook office had a phone. This kind of association can be very useful, which is why it's important to stay aware of what is going on in your district. It was certainly the deciding factor for me, and a phone line was installed the following week. It's important to note that I wouldn't have become angry if my principal had said no, and I certainly wouldn't have given up. Asking the principal was just the first step.

Years ago, I read a book called *Games People Play* by Eric Berne (1996). I found the ideas in this book very useful in dealing with students, teachers, parents, and administrators, even though it was not written specifically for educators. One of the games it describes is called "Wooden Leg." People who play this game always have excuses for their inability to do something they want or need to do. For example, they may say, "I could really teach history if it weren't for these awful kids," or "I could try some more interesting things in my classes if it weren't for the administrators," or "There'd be no stopping me if I could only get the money from the school board," and on and on. It is true that sometimes great ideas are stifled because of lack of funds or support, but I don't believe in making excuses. Teachers help, we are not helpless; we are leaders who can make things happen. Complaining doesn't solve the situation, and it makes the whiner look impotent to the other staff members.

> It will save you much wasted effort if you can figure out what is out of your control and then stop worrying about it.

I have a large poster of the famous serenity prayer that reminds us that true wisdom is knowing the difference between the things we can do something about and the things we can't do anything about. Many of the novels we read in class clearly illustrate this philosophy. I tell my students they are not victims and they can choose whether or not to live with a problem. When you're working in a school, it saves you much wasted effort if you can figure out what is out of your control and then stop worrying about it. In the same manner, figure out what is within your control and take some action.

Another game described in *Games People Play* (Berne, 1996) is called "Yes, but . . . ." It goes like this. Someone comes to you with a problem and you offer several possible solutions. However, after each recommendation, the other person says, "Yes, but . . ." and tells you why he or she can't do what you've suggested. I will play this game through three "Yes, buts," and then I realize that the person does not want to solve the problem; he or she just wants to complain about it. I offer to be a sounding board if and when my colleague comes up with an idea, and then I move on. I don't like to feed into the negative attitude or the sense of wallowing. I honestly believe there's always a solution.

> *Every problem has a solution; sometimes we need to be a little more clever or look at it from a totally different perspective.*

I have a friend who is a firm believer in visualization—physically and mentally creating a very specific image of what it is you want. She believes that when you become this focused, what you need will come to you. It's happened many times in her life. This doesn't mean that you just sit around and wish. Quite often, I've stumbled on solutions to problems by mentioning what I need to a wide variety of people. The people who work in schools can be amazingly resourceful, and you'll be surprised at the connections they have outside the system. Some of the most valuable resources available to you are the janitors, maintenance personnel, and secretaries in your school. They know far more than you ever will about what is going on in the district, and they can make your life a lot easier.

Students and parents will also amaze you. In the days when students needed to do paste-up to produce a newspaper, I wanted to build another light table for my journalism class but couldn't find a piece of glass thick enough. I mentioned this to my senior English students and one boy shouted, "My daddy works for Ford Motors—we'll get you that glass!" I've had students bring in computers, printer paper, and other office supplies donated by their parents. (I always double-check with their folks to make sure it really is "donated.") I've asked parents to speak to classes about their professions, and sometimes they connect me with someone who works in a field my students are researching. I've also had many useful items donated by community businesses that are glad to support local schools. I practice what I preach to my students and write letters to anyone who can possibly help me do the best job I can. When a letter is answered, I share it with my students to point out the power of the written word. The worst thing that can happen is *not* that the request is denied; the worst thing that can happen is that you didn't try.

If you're a new teacher, listen to students, teachers, and other personnel talk about what's going on in other classes in your school district. Fairly soon you'll hear someone's name come up over and over because the students are working on innovative projects or because that person is involved in the decision-making processes of the school. Go to this teacher and ask for help. I guarantee that 99% of the time, the teacher will be delighted to share information, materials, and advice. Some schools have a mentoring system in place already, but if your school doesn't, find your own mentor. I've had teachers sit in on my classes during their planning periods to observe the system I've created or to learn how to work with students with learning disabilities or behavior problems. This has never bothered me, and I'm honored they asked. I believe in being helpful to everyone I can because I know I'll need help in the future myself. I've cleared some of my biggest hurdles by calling in favors from people I've helped in the past. Online discussion forums make it fairly simple to connect with people working in the same field as you who may have practical answers to your questions. Every problem has a solution; sometimes we need to be a little more clever or look at it from a totally different perspective. The fifth commandment of good teaching? Ask and ye just may receive.

6

Thou Shalt Be Fair and Prepared

A few strong instincts and a few plain rules.

—William Wordsworth

Now that you have your vision, your lesson plans, and the equipment you need, how do you get your captive audience to sit down and be captivated? Discipline is the biggest challenge you face in the classroom, and it is surely the Achilles' heel of most new teachers. I've been teaching for many, many years, and you can tell that I love my job. However, when I started out, I wanted to quit because I was sure I'd never get the students to behave. It was without a doubt my weakest point. Now, I consider it one of my strengths. What happened?

In the beginning, I did not understand the nature of power or control. Like most new teachers, I started out trying to recreate the classrooms I had seen as a student. I had heard all the advice that has been passed down for generations about not smiling until Christmas, starting out tough but easing up as the class progresses, and showing the kids as much respect as they show you. These gems may work for some people, but they were useless for me. I had two problems with this advice from the beginning: (1) I wanted the students to enjoy my class, and (2) I remembered what I did as a kid to teachers who were inflexible control freaks.

In my experience, mere force just doesn't work. My problem was that the kids would behave fairly well for a while, but they would push for more and more freedom, and the class would end in chaos with both the students and me glad to see the other leave. I often left school in tears and dreaded going back the next day. After a great deal of experience, I realized I was doing two things wrong. First, the students could tell I was apologetic that we had rules and unsure about what I was doing. Second, I made threats I didn't back up. The students saw right through me, and human nature being what it is, they wrestled for control of the class. What was interesting was that none of us were very happy about the situation. This was my first clue: Children like to know there is someone in charge—someone who has their best interests at heart and who has a plan. I grew up hating rules, but I came to realize there are very few human interactions that can function without them.

> *Children like to know there is someone in charge—someone who has their best interests at heart and who has a plan.*

Some time ago, one of my reading classes was not going well. Partly because of the mix of students in the class, many of whom had learning and behavioral disabilities, I felt I was spending more time than usual just keeping the kids in line. Instead of placing blame or coming down on the students with an iron fist, I found a solution where I least expected it. I was reading the monthly magazine of the National Education Association, which showcases what teachers across America are doing in their classrooms. In it was a short profile of a history teacher with a unique way of getting his students to understand the need for laws in this country. A light went on in my head, and I planned a similar activity for the next day. As the reading students filed into the room, I waited until they were all seated and told them that I'd been unhappy with the way the class was going. This caused a sigh, and they all took the slumping posture of students who know they are about to be chewed out by an authority figure. I said I considered it my fault (faces shot up all over the room) and I realized I had been too rule-oriented and needed to lighten things up (suspicion rippled in their eyes). I suggested that instead of getting right into our regular work, we should play a game. I had everyone stand up and form a large circle around the room. Meanwhile, I pulled a beach ball out from behind my desk. Without giving any directions, I threw the ball at a student. He looked at me, puzzled, but I just smiled and said, "Go ahead!" He shrugged his shoulders and threw the ball at another student. Ignoring the comments about my sanity, I arbitrarily pointed at a student and commanded him or her to sit down. I continued to do this after every few tosses of the ball, and soon only one boy was left standing. I congratulated him on being the winner and asked him if he wanted to play again. He told me that this was the most ignorant game he'd ever played. I looked hurt and asked him why— I'd had fun. He pointed out that no one knew what to do; they were all just throwing a stupid ball. Another chimed in that there was no winner because they didn't know what I expected. I looked confused and asked what they meant. Bless his heart, one of the most rebellious students in the class shouted out, "We couldn't play right because there were no rules." The last word kind of died on his lips because even though he was one of the most infamous behavior problems in the school, he was also quite smart. I grinned and innocently asked, "So, you're saying that for a group of people to enjoy themselves, we need some guidelines?" The point was quickly taken, and we had a good talk about the rules of my class and the logic behind them. As students moved to join their groups, I heard one of them say, "I told you she was tricky."

Your class needs rules, but they have to be your rules, based on what creates order in your room and enhances the learning experience. In one of my schools, every teacher was required to submit an assertive discipline plan to the vice-principal at the beginning of the semester. New teachers were given a sample copy to use, and it amazed me how many of them just copied down the generic rules and consequences and turned those in. Granted, there are some tried-and-true rules that work well, such as "Come prepared to work." That covers a lot of territory, from bringing supplies to paying attention. But only an inexperienced teacher would put "No talking" on a rule sheet. That is a setup for failure.

How do I know? Well, let's go back to my best training ground for teaching—my old high school. I once had a teacher who taught English and home economics, and unfortunately for her, I was in both classes. This woman gave the impression of being nervous and angry, and she definitely did not understand the nature of control. I figured I had sized her up within the first 10 minutes of class, and she seemed like fair game. She had yelled at several students already, including me, and I knew she'd be an easy mark.

> *Your class needs rules, but they have to be your rules, based on what creates order in your room and enhances the learning experience.*

As expected, she sat us in rows and she stood at the front behind a teacher's station, a barrier that seemed highly symbolic at the time. I used my usual strategy of sitting in the back of the class and hiding behind someone with big hair. This gave me a lot of leeway. She had the rules of her class posted on the front wall, and the minute I saw "No talking" and "Do not get up out of your seat," I knew I was home free. The first time she turned her back to write something on the board, I tossed my pen about three feet from my desk then waved my hand frantically in the air. When she turned around, she eyed me with disgust and asked what I wanted. I smiled and innocently asked her to please come pick up my pen for me because I was just trying to follow her rules, and I couldn't ask the person next to me because we couldn't talk, and I couldn't get it myself because we couldn't get out of our seats and would she please get it for me so I could continue taking notes? The class froze as her eyes narrowed and blood started rushing to her cheeks, but she knew I had her. Glaring at me, she marched to the back of the room, picked up my pen, and slammed it on my desk. I smiled my most angelic smile and thanked her profusely. As she made her way back to the front, I tossed the pen three feet in the other direction. When she turned around to continue her lecture, there I was waving my hand again. By now her voice was cracking with anger when she asked what I wanted this time. I acted all flustered and said I didn't know what was wrong with me, maybe I was just so excited to be back in school or something, but I dropped my pen again and would she please come get it for me because I couldn't talk and I couldn't get out of my seat. That did it. She screamed, "Come with me, young lady!" and marched me down to the principal's office. The class was thrilled because they'd have around 10 or 15 teacher-free minutes, and most of my classmates fondly waved goodbye as I left. When we got to the office, the teacher told the principal that I was acting up in class, and he asked me to tell him what I'd done. I looked puzzled and said, "I don't know, I was just trying to follow her rules. She told us we couldn't talk or get out of our seats, and I dropped my pen and asked her to get it for me." He turned to the teacher and asked if that was true. She kind of sputtered, "Yes, no, yes, but no!" What could she say? She made the rules. I spent many hours sitting in the hall outside of her class as the semester progressed, but I didn't care—I usually had a good book with me. She thought she was punishing me, but I was thrilled that I didn't have to sit and listen to her. Never for a moment did she convince me that she had anything to teach me. I wasn't the only student to give her problems, and she left the profession after only a couple of years.

I don't want this to happen to you, so here are some rules for making up rules. First, go back to your vision for your class and think about what behaviors would inhibit learning—anticipation is everything. Second, physically set up your class to avoid problems before they get there. Spread the students out as much as you can, and allow for unobtrusive movement in the room. Third, make sure whatever consequence you choose for breaking a rule makes sense, and make sure you're willing to enforce it. Never threaten. Fourth, design a number of activities to help the students develop a sense of purpose and community about your class. Students are not as likely to act inappropriately if they feel they are important members of a team with common goals. Finally, spend some time demonstrating to your students why you have the specific rules in place, how the consequences are logical, and what the rewards will be. The students should definitely have the idea that you have rules in your class not for some false sense of power, but to simplify things and eliminate chaos. The rules help them.

I mentioned earlier that one of the hardest parts of being a teacher is that you are a constant role model. When you deal with your students, you show them how to solve problems. You can talk all you want, but they pay attention to what you do. When you yell and scream at a class, do not be surprised when they yell and scream back at you. If you show them little respect, don't be surprised when they show you none. A teacher who controls a class through threats and accusations had better never turn her back. This kind of power is no power at all. All of us can physically make a student do something—we may have to call in a bigger teacher or an administrator—but there's no trick to making a kid shut up and sit down. It's keeping him or her there that's difficult.

As a student, if I want to get out of working in your class, I'll just kick up dust and distract you. That teacher who dragged me to the office so many years ago thought she had power over me, but as a teen, I felt like I was in control of the situation. I successfully delayed her lesson for at least 20 minutes and made her look like a fool in front of her students and her principal. Sure, she gave me an F, but at the time I was rather proud of my collection of failing grades. One way I can tell when teachers are struggling is that they have a high percentage of Fs in their grade book. How hard is that? What's difficult is to have a high percentage of students succeed. Can you think of another business in the world where workers can fail to turn out half their products and keep their jobs? Only in education. Failing a student is not a sign of power; it's an admission of defeat. I do not believe in giving away passing grades; that is also a sign of false power and a shocking lack of faith. But over and over I see new, as well as experienced, teachers using grades to punish students. Kids who are serious behavior problems probably have a string of Fs on their belts—it means nothing to them. Many of them are used to conflict in the classroom and are so out of control at home, your threat doesn't even faze them.

> *Failing a student is not a sign of power; it's an admission of defeat.*

One of our main goals as teachers should be to help students learn self-discipline, and we can't accomplish this if the only control we understand comes from the person in the position of authority. I have a way of making my students understand the true nature of power. I pick the biggest guy in the group and tell him that I can force him to stay in my class. The kids kind of chuckle when I tell the student to try to leave, but it is impossible because I'm between him and the door. I stand behind the kid and (with his permission) push down on his shoulders, saying in a strained voice, "Okay, now try to leave—you can't do it because I'm too strong." Everyone laughs when the student easily throws off my hands and heads for the door. I act stunned and ask the group what went wrong. They quickly point out that he was bigger and stronger and wanted to leave. I nod and say, "All right, physical force didn't work; even if I could have held him there, my power over him depends on me not getting tired. Let's try something else." This time I sit down next to the boy, tell him that I will spend the next few months doing everything in my power to help him succeed in his goals, that I am really glad he's in my class, and that I've got all sorts of interesting things to teach him.

Then I ask if he'd like to stay. He always says yes, and I point out that no one in the room could force him to leave now because he wants to be there. The choice is his rather than mine—the key is to move the class as soon as possible from teacher control to self-control. The kids behave because they want to be there.

During the first week of a school year, I spend about 10 minutes every day discussing the rules, consequences, and rewards of the class. I have a list of general rules that I type into a simple contract that is signed and dated by the students on the second day of school. Right now, the five rules in my class are:

1. Be on time.

2. No food or drinks in the classroom except bottled water.

3. Don't disturb other students.

4. Follow directions.

5. Come prepared to work.

The first two are school-wide rules and need little explanation, but the other three are more general, and I spend some time explaining specifically what I mean by each. Rule 3 is the most important on the list. Thinking back to my high school experience, I know that it is possible to enforce "Don't disturb other students" and I avoid falling into the "Don't get out of your seats" and "No talking" traps. Students talk in class—you want them to. Some students, especially those with attention deficit hyperactivity disorder (ADHD), find it difficult to sit for long periods of time. Sometimes, all they need to do is walk across the room to throw away a piece of paper—just make sure you place the trash can at the back of the room so they can be as unobtrusive as possible. What you don't want is for their talking or movement to disturb others and inhibit the learning process. I have known students who were put in detention because they leaned over and asked their neighbor what page they were on. There's a big difference between this and a kid talking so loudly that no one can hear what anyone else is saying. To help them understand exactly what I mean, I set up a scenario where I'm listening to a nearby student read his essay to me—I act enthralled by his clever use of diction and syntax. Without shifting my gaze, I say, "Then suddenly Megan does something that makes me go like this" and my eyes shoot across the room to little Megan, who usually jumps a few inches out of her seat. The kids laugh, but the point is made. Productive talking or movement is fine with me, but something that breaks my or my students' attention from where it should be is a disturbance and is not acceptable.

> It's been my experience that every minute you spend on setting up, explaining, and acting out the class rules will save you hours of time dealing with disciplinary problems during the rest of the school year.

Rule 4, "Follow directions," covers anything from paying attention to the group schedule to playing games on the computers. One of the questions on the rules quiz they take at the end of the first week asks them to specifically list what they may or may not do on the computers: They can use the computers to work on projects or assignments that relate to our class, but they may not check their e-mail, MySpace page, or play games like solitaire. One of the first directions I give is to keep working until I dismiss the class; they are not allowed to pack up their things and stand by the door waiting for the bell to ring, even if only 30 seconds remain in the class period. I am always teaching or working with a small group of students, and it's easy for my students to understand how distracting that would be. The last rule, "Come prepared to work," alludes to an attitude—a work ethic—and includes showing up with the necessary materials and homework. Every once in a while I have a student who provocatively asks, "If we're done with our work, can we sleep?" I smile benevolently and say, "Of course, but only when I'm done with my work and I sleep." I present the rules with a sense of humor, but also with a sense of authority. I take time to make sure that everyone understands what I'm asking them to do and why I'm asking them to do it. Each student signs the contract at the bottom— the last line says, "I have read and understand the rules" rather than "I agree with the rules." By the time they take a quiz with 10 short-answer questions about the rules and consequences, the tone is set, and the students and I are confident about my expectations. It's been my experience that every minute you spend on setting up, explaining, and acting out the class rules will save you hours of time dealing with disciplinary problems during the rest of the school year.

Obviously, it's not enough to hand the kids a list of rules; you must have a simple set of specific actions that you'll take if a student chooses to break a class rule. The consequences of breaking the rules in my class are the same for all but being tardy. That's a general school rule, and the principal takes care of that consequence: a letter is sent home after the third tardy, students serve a detention after the sixth tardy. For all the other rules, I give a verbal warning, quickly and quietly reminding them of what they should be doing. If they ignore the verbal warning, I ask them to write a Reflective Essay. The way I present this is by saying that it would be rare for someone to have such a bad day that they choose to continue an action that interrupted the learning process, but it could happen. In that case, it would be helpful for the student to reflect on the problem his or her behavior caused. This is the paragraph that appears right below the list of rules and consequences on the contract the students sign:

> A student who is having problems remembering the rules of the class will write a 250-word essay reflecting on the causes and effects of the infraction, as well as a plan of action for avoiding the problem in the future. The essay must be turned in at the beginning of the next class meeting. If the essay is one day late, it will expand to 500 words. If the expanded essay is not turned in at the beginning of the

next class meeting, the student will be sent to the office to meet with the principal. The student may return to class when the essay is completed.

A clever student will notice that when the Reflective Essay is turned in, the teacher has a signed and dated account of the infraction in the student's own words. This consequence is not so punitive that I hesitate to enforce it, but it's annoying enough that the students don't want to face it. On the average, I hand out one or two Reflective Essays a year.

> *One of the best ways to eliminate discipline problems is to have a reputation as a good teacher who tries to make learning enjoyable but who will do what she says she is going to do.*

So what are the rewards for following the rules? Well, the students get to be in my class. I know this sounds conceited, but one of the best ways to eliminate discipline problems is to have a reputation as a good teacher who works to make learning meaningful and enjoyable but who will do what she says she is going to do. After a year or two, students will be predisposed to behave in your class because they have heard from your former students and your colleagues how much they enjoy your class. I don't believe in giving movies or free days as rewards because these have been overused. I tell the students their main rewards are that authentic learning occurs in this class and everything we do is designed to make them successful in the future. I also compliment them often on their good behavior; if I say it often—only when it's true—that will be how they perceive themselves. I have given them that image of themselves. Never, even once, say to a class, "You guys are great, but that Period 2! They're my worst class." It will get back to the kids in Period 2, and they will cheerfully embrace the label and live down to your expectations.

When I review the rules two days before the quiz, I role-play to make sure that everyone understands exactly what happens when we break into groups the following week. From the minute they walk into my class at the beginning of the year, I take note of the kids with attitudes or the ones who overtly call attention to themselves. Even though I don't know them yet, these kids are fairly easy to spot. I tell the students that we're going to go over the rules and consequences one more time to make sure there are no misunderstandings so they'll all earn A's on tomorrow's test. Then I innocently pick one of the potential troublemakers and say, "Let's say it's next week and everyone is in groups, working away. I'm up at the board getting ready to work with my group. I turn around and (gasp) Joe is sitting there talking with Julie! He's supposed to be on the computers! I'm stunned, but I figure he just lost track of the time. I say, 'Joe, you need to get on the computers,' and naturally he smiles, gives me a nod, and gets right to work. He's a great guy. But let's pretend, and I know that this would never happen, but let's pretend that Joe is just having a really bad day and I look up again, and he's still sitting there talking to Julie. I can barely believe my eyes I'm so shocked, but I quietly walk over and put a Reflective Essay worksheet on his desk. I figure he didn't realize the impact his actions had on our class, so it will give him a chance to mull it over."

Then, I turn to the class in general and ask, "When I give Joe the Reflective Essay, what does he say?" This usually causes general snickers because Joe probably has a history of fighting with teachers, but I break in and say, "Joe says, 'Thank you, Ms. Gill. Thank you for giving me this because you told me that if I ignored your verbal warning that's what would happen. I even signed a paper saying I understood the consequence, so I want to thank you for being the kind of person who does what she says she's going to do—the kind of person I can trust—bless your heart!'" By now the class is howling, including Joe, but the point is made. There's no arguing when a teacher asks a student to fulfill the consequence of breaking a rule because the student agreed to it ahead of time to stay in the class, and the teacher said that this is what she would do.

The next day, we role-play again using a different student, and we practice doubling the essay to 500 words and heading on down to the office. Again, I point out that the student will probably be thanking me profusely as we walk down the hall because I'm the kind of person who keeps her word. I'm not the type of teacher who is in a good mood one day so the class can get away with anything, but the next day is in a bad mood and everyone is in trouble. At the end of the week, they take a quiz on the rules, and this is the first grade of the semester. Most students get a perfect score, which lets me know that they understand completely what I expect. When I hand back the tests, I can clear up any confusion, and by the time we break into groups the following week, the class runs pretty smoothly. I keep a photocopy of the signed rules contract and the quiz in a folder for documentation in case some students tell an administrator or parent that they had no idea they had to bring the Reflective Essay in the next day. Spending 10 or 15 minutes every day at the beginning of the year lets the students know how seriously I take my responsibility for protecting the positive learning environment in our classroom.

> *Just as I don't mind stopping at a traffic light, most students understand that rules are designed to protect them and to create an optimum learning environment.*

I rarely take a student to the office—once a year at the most. When I do, the student is in some serious trouble because it's such a rare occurrence. There are teachers in my school who average one student to the principal per class period. I'm not sure if they do this to scare the students or to get out of embarrassing situations, but it's a huge mistake. It sends the wrong message to two very important groups of people. One, it gives administrators the impression the teacher cannot handle the students. Two, it lets the students know the teacher is not the bottom line; it's the administrators who count. I handle almost all my disciplinary problems myself—the students know it's between the two of us and it will be solved. I do ask advice from counselors and other teachers to find out background information that may give me clues as to why students are acting up in class.

When creating a discipline plan for your class, do the following:

1. Anticipate possible problems ahead of time.

2. Create an internal system allowing students to control most of their own behavior.

3. Be sure your rules are logical and can be enforced.

4. Spend quite a bit of time reviewing the rules and consequences so there is no doubt in anyone's mind about what you expect.

5. Do what you say you will do every time in as matter-of-fact a manner as possible.

Just as I don't mind stopping at a traffic light, most students understand that rules are designed to protect them and to create an optimum learning environment. The sixth commandment of good teaching? Thou shalt be fair and prepared for problems before they get there.

7

Thou Shalt Use Some Common Sense

Laws too gentle are seldom obeyed; too severe, seldom executed.

—Benjamin Franklin

I've spent a great deal of time telling you about the specific set of rules and consequences I've designed for my class. I have to run a pretty tight ship because of the small amount of time I have to work with each of the groups. However, teaching is a people business, and stuff happens. There are times when you have to make a judgment call based on old-fashioned common sense. Every rule has an exception, and you have to develop instincts to be able to read a situation quickly enough to defuse it before it gets out of hand. By working with your students as individually as possible, you can get fairly adept at separating the trustworthy kids from the manipulators.

There are very few times I allow a student to sit and do nothing in my class. The kids just know they have to work all period long because that's what I expect. But occasionally, a student comes in who is obviously agitated and at the breaking point. Something may have happened at home or in the last class, and this kid is ready to blow. If I see this, I'll sit next to him or her while the other students move around getting into the groups. I'll try to get the troubled student to tell me what is wrong, but sometimes, he or she won't talk or—even worse—the student will scream at me. Right then I have to make a decision. I hope I know enough about this student to guess what's wrong. Based on my instincts, I'll take the student into the hall to talk, take the student to the office to talk to someone else, or leave him or her alone to cool down. The one thing I know I *won't* do is take the anger personally. This child may scream that he or she hates me, but unless I've done something on purpose to make this kid mad, I'm not going to react to the words. This is just misplaced rage, and I'd be a fool to buy into it by losing my temper, too.

> *Every rule has an exception, and you have to develop instincts to be able to read a situation quickly enough to defuse it before it gets out of hand.*

Remember, the teacher is the role model. I'm not going to show my students the same amount of respect they show me; because I'm the adult, I'll actually show them far more respect, so they can learn by example. Sometimes students tell me I give them too much work or they don't feel like doing anything. I could tell them to sit down and shut up or I'll flunk them. I guess that's one approach. But I usually say, "I give you a lot of work because I care about you. If I didn't respect you, I'd let you sit there and do nothing." I'm the one who sets the tone for the class and treats them better than I expect to be treated.

Another tool in my arsenal is a fine-tuned "crap detector." I describe this to the students as a little alarm inside me that goes off when I hear something that doesn't add up. I tell them this is one of the most powerful resources they can develop to help them in just about any situation they're likely to encounter. As the semester progresses, I'll call a group up to meet with me and someone won't have the work done. This person begins an elaborate story about dogs and homework and a best friend's broken-down car. I'll listen politely, then toward the end, I'll look startled and say, "Did you hear that?" The kids start looking around. I'll turn my head toward the student and say, "Yep, beep, beep, beep, my crap detector just went off." Usually, everyone starts laughing, including the kid with the excuses. A few years ago, one of my students gave me a headline he'd torn from the newspaper. It said "The Best Crap Detector in the USA." I proudly pasted it to the front of my roll book and sometimes all I need to do is hold it up and point to it.

Another book I find very useful is *Games Students Play* by Ken Ernst (1974). Many students have developed some rather clever strategies over the years to outwit teachers—I know I was a major player in high school. One I see all the time is called "Uproar." It goes like this: a student demands to leave the room at an inappropriate time to go to the restroom. The teacher tells the student no. The student starts arguing, insisting it's an emergency and creating such a fuss that the teacher lets him or her go just to get the student out of the room. Even if the student is not allowed to leave, the teacher makes a mental note that this kid can create quite an uproar. The next time the student makes an unreasonable demand, the teacher gives in to avoid the scene that's sure to follow. This is probably how that student has been training teachers (as well as parents) for years. If you spot an Uproar player, never confront him or her in front of the whole class. Make one of those quick decisions either to ignore it for the time being or to take the student into the hallway. When you get the student alone, call him or her on the game. Without a trace of anger in your voice, tell the student you didn't realize that he or she was an Uproar player and you're glad you found out. Smile, nod knowingly, and say you recognize this is how the student has controlled teachers for years, but luckily for him or her, you are a teacher who understands this game and won't play. Quickly explain why you wouldn't let the student leave the class and how you'd like to handle the same situation in the future. Before you return to class, tell the student you're glad he or she is there, but because you have so much to accomplish, you just can't have any outbursts like that. This may sound naive to you, but it really works. Remember to handle all discipline problems as matter-of-factly as possible. It's not personal.

Because you're learning to anticipate problems before they occur, you need to develop a simple system for allowing students to leave your class to use the restroom. This may seem ridiculous, but I've noticed this can become one of the biggest fights that leads to an angry teacher and an angrier student to the principal's office. Refusing to allow students to use the restroom during a 90-minute class is setting yourself up for some serious battles—with parents as well as students. It is almost impossible to tell whether a student really has to go, so don't even play that game. I taught for a year next door to a new teacher who was having a horrible time making his students behave. I could literally hear desks being thrown against the wall, and I went over a couple of times, but it embarrassed the teacher so much that I stopped doing it. The principal tried to intervene a number of times, but the kids would calm down when she came in, so things appeared to be in control. I offered to help in any way I could, but the teacher was afraid to let anyone know how much trouble he was having because he thought he could lose his job as a result. He was fired anyway. In a desperate attempt to control his students, he forbade anyone to leave the class under any circumstances. In his defense, he had students leaving four and five times within an hour to "use the bathroom." He told them they had abused the privilege, so he was taking it away. I was horrified to learn later in the year that one student had urinated in the corner of the room because he said he couldn't hold it any longer. This shows how out of control things can get when a teacher creates a rule that can't be enforced.

> *Many of your students will have developed some rather clever strategies over the years to outwit teachers.*

In my class, the students are free to leave the class once per period if they need to use the restroom. I don't ask them where they're going, but they know they have to follow the regular school rules. I leave the hall pass on a counter by the door. They have to sign out, stating where they're going, when they left, and when they returned. I tell them that they cannot leave when their small group is working with me. The only other requirement is that they enter and exit so quietly that no one notices. It works fairly smoothly, and it's rare that a student abuses the system, but if that happens, instead of getting angry, I ask the student to stay after class to find out if there is a medical problem of some sort—using the words "doctor" and "call home" convinces the kid not to take advantage of the situation. The best advice I can give is to pick and choose your fights. Arguing about whether the students legitimately need to use the restroom is not one I choose to take on.

It's been my experience that people have a great deal of control over how others react to them. There's no question that teachers set the tone for their classes and sometimes cause problems themselves. Many years ago, I read *Transactional Analysis in Psychotherapy* (1961) by Eric Berne, the author of *Games People Play* (1996). In this book, Berne describes a system of behavioral modification called transactional analysis (TA). I found this especially helpful in developing my instincts for dealing with students. In fact, I teach a mini-unit in TA to my students because it's so useful in explaining why people respond to us so differently. According to TA, each of us has learned how to be a parent, an adult, and a child by observing the behavior of the significant people in our lives. I tell my students that from the moment they are born, a little recorder turns on in their heads. We record these, without evaluating, what it is to be a parent by watching our guardians,

> *There's no question that teachers set the tone for their classes and sometimes cause problems themselves.*

what it is to be an adult by watching the few we run into, and we experience naturally what it is to be a child. According to Berne, we all have a part of us that reacts like a Critical Parent, a Nurturing Parent, an Adult, a Submissive Child, a Rebellious Child, and a Free Child. Depending on the personalities of the significant role models in our lives, we may have more information about one than another. For example, a student who was abandoned or poorly cared for as a child does not react very often in a Nurturing Parent manner because that's just not something he or she observed while growing up. Someone who grew up under the thumb of a Critical Parent either learned to be submissive to survive or possibly fought back in a rebellious manner.

I try to get students to analyze themselves and focus on how they most often react to other people. I also point out that many of the "transactional states" are symbiotic. For example, the Nurturing Parent in us can trigger the Submissive Child in others. Think how this works in a classroom. Teachers who choose to control their students through threats and constant put-downs, the modus operandi of the Critical Parent, naturally recognize and respond negatively to the Rebellious Child in many of their students. Ultimately, the teacher is the one who fuels the conflict by not understanding what is going on. There is no way I'm going to get into a head-on confrontation with a Rebellious Child. I may win a few battles, but I'll surely lose the war. In the same manner, I'm not about to stay in my Nurturing Parent when dealing with my students. Even though this may bring out their submissive natures, it also makes them dependent on me and, therefore, they remain in a childlike state. It doesn't help to pity or become codependent with a struggling kid—we need to empower them, not to cover for them. The logical place to stay in most of our relationships at school is in our Adults. This is the part of us that makes decisions based on the best information available rather than emotional responses. The Adult in the teacher tends to bring out the Adult in the students. I would encourage anyone who deals with people on a professional basis to read Berne's book. I have used the TA techniques with great success with my students and with my own children.

Many people who become educators were good students in school. They were often well mannered and always had their work done on time. Some of these students go on to become remarkable teachers. However, I've noticed that teachers who never had to struggle to learn or to control their behavior tend to have little tolerance for the students who do. Whenever I conduct workshops for English teachers, I make them laugh by pointing out that if I were to tell them to get out a piece of paper right now because we're going to write for 30 minutes, most of them would say, "Oh, goody," and get right to it. But I know many adults (and kids) who would say, "Kill me now—just put me out of my misery!" We may have loved writing or solving math problems when we were young, but many students find these tasks so frustrating and wrought with failure that they will do whatever they can to keep the teacher from moving forward with the lesson. As teachers, we have to be sensitive to the fact that few of our students learn in the same manner as we do, and we have to learn to accommodate for these differences. Frustrated, embarrassed students will usually become behavior problems. You need to develop a set of rules by which to run your classes, but sometimes you will be called on to make decisions based on your instincts rather than the normal solutions. The seventh commandment of good teaching? When making choices that affect your students, thou shalt use some common sense.

Frustrated, embarrassed students will usually become behavior problems.

8

Thou Shalt Be Open-Minded and Flexible

We had the experience but missed the meaning.

—T. S. Eliot

Teachers are natural-born leaders. We have to be, but this is also the reason why some faculty meetings can be such unpleasant experiences. It isn't just that we have to stay after school or get up early to attend the meeting; it's that the room is full of highly opinionated, pushy people who are used to telling others what to do. In all human beings, the quality that is our greatest strength can also be our greatest weakness. There is a fine line between being decisive and being overbearing, between being in charge and being a martinet. When the bell rings and the door closes to the classroom, we're the boss. One of my favorite things about teaching is that no one is looking over my shoulder telling me what to do. The quality of what goes on in my classroom is solely in my hands.

However, I don't teach in isolation. I am part of a professional learning community, and I'm responsible for that group as well. I constantly wrestle with the impulse to stay in my room and ignore the rest of the world. Sometimes, I'll pass a classroom where the students are obviously out of control and the teacher is struggling. What I most want to do is turn my head and move on. But at my best, I realize that all the students in the school are my students and I have an obligation to at least offer to help in as nonjudgmental a way as possible.

Teaching can be the loneliest profession in the world. When I first began teaching in Tennessee, the principal handed me a roll book and a key to my room and wished me luck. I didn't know how to take attendance or that teachers would be expected to buy most of their supplies, such as chalk. Except with one advanced English class, I struggled through that year, and no one on the staff paid any attention to my situation. I was too embarrassed to admit I was having problems because I thought that would make me appear incompetent. My family had just moved to the area from California, and I didn't know a soul. It was the closest I've come to quitting the profession. I had a terrible year because no one offered to help and I didn't ask. Most of the teachers I know have had similar experiences and tend to be very kind about looking out for a newcomer.

> *I am part of a professional learning community, and I'm responsible for that group as well. I constantly wrestle with the impulse to stay in my room.*

On the other hand, keep in mind that teachers are also an opinionated lot who offer advice even when it isn't requested. Even after all of these years, I have to remind myself that few of us teach in the same way. Schools are filled with all types of personalities and styles. I think I do a good job as an educator, but I have had students who I feel gained little from being in my class. Either they couldn't handle the freedom inherent in my system or they found my earnestness obnoxious. They responded far better to a more structured teacher who lectured for most of the period. We all have different teaching and learning styles, and we should honor those. The bottom line is whether or not the way you present information and manage your class accomplishes your goals.

One of the biggest traps a teacher can fall into is to spend even a small amount of time worrying or griping about what teachers down the hall are or aren't doing. First, unless they request your input, it's none of your business. However, if their classes are so chaotic they disturb your class, that's a different story. The first step is to speak to the individual teacher, explain the problem, and offer any assistance you can. The second step is to talk to an administrator about the problem, but this should occur only if what other teachers are doing interferes with what you are trying to do.

I have been asked to serve on faculty advisory committees over the years, but I usually decline. The members of this committee are chosen by the faculty to present their concerns to the principal in regular monthly meetings. The idea behind it is to save time and to allow a teacher to bring up a sensitive issue anonymously. In some schools, this committee can be a powerful force to help steer the school toward a collective vision. In other schools, the meetings can disintegrate into rather lengthy gripe sessions. In my experience, 90% of the discussions were either complaints about other faculty members or someone wanted to vent about situations that were unsolvable because of budget constraints. Very few were suggestions or solutions. Whenever you bring up an issue in a group meeting, make sure that it's something that can be solved by those present. If it concerns one or two other people, make an appointment to speak with the responsible administrator in private. It's a waste of everyone's time to just complain or feed into rumors; more important, this negativity is self-perpetuating and can sap the sense of collegiality among the staff.

Earlier in this book, I encouraged you to ask when you need something, but be careful what you ask for because you might get it. For example, I've known teachers who spend an inordinate amount of time worrying about what other teachers wear to school. In one of my schools, they demanded the principal do something about the unprofessional style of dress of some colleagues, so the principal offered to set up a very rigid dress code for all teachers. These same teachers were outraged—they didn't want someone dictating what they could or couldn't wear; they primarily wanted to complain. Years ago, I heard a story about a two-year-old boy, sucking on a pacifier, who was sitting next to his mother. The mother was talking with a large group of women who were planning a party. One of the women kept staring at the boy and finally said, "What in the world are you doing sucking on that pacifier, a big boy like you? That's for babies." The little boy took the pacifier out of his mouth, looked the woman straight in the eye, and said, "Hurts you?" I can't tell you how often this saying runs through my head when I'm listening to teachers complain about one another. I want to ask, "Hurts you?"

> *We have to learn to pick and choose our battles.*

Every year, we have a summer faculty meeting during which we discuss plans for the upcoming school year. Without exception someone brings up the shocking state of student dress and demands a strictly enforced dress code. This usually results in an hour-long debate over the finer issues, such as how baggy can pants be before they're outlawed? How short is too short for a skirt or top? The trouble is that most of these teachers can't define their terms. When I first moved to Tennessee, I was surprised to hear that boys were not allowed to wear tank tops but girls were. In my first faculty meeting, I naively asked what was wrong with tank tops and was told that some of the teachers just couldn't stand to see underarm hair. I didn't know how to respond to that; it seemed so ridiculous. We have to learn to pick and choose our battles, and a student dress code is one that screams for common sense. The other teachers know that I pay very little attention to what my students wear because my focus is on their faces to make sure they understand what I'm saying. They'd have to be dressed in something pretty outrageous for me to notice.

This debate has gone on so long that when the dress code issue is brought up in a meeting, everyone turns to hear me declare my ultra-radical, bleeding-heart opposition to strict rules dictating how the kids dress. But what I say year after year seems like common sense to me. If what a student is wearing interferes with the learning environment, send that student out of class to change. For that matter, if what a teacher is wearing interferes with the learning environment, that teacher should change. That's it. Sure, this requires judgment calls, but that's why we're the highly respected professionals we're paid to be. I personally wouldn't mind students wearing hats in my class unless the brim covers their eyes. If that were the case, I would tell them to take the hat off or turn it around. This is not a big problem. But I have known teachers to waste half a class period in the office with a student who may or may not have on pants that sag too low. One of the most disgusting scenes I've observed as a teacher was two male administrators on their knees in front of a 16-year-old girl measuring the length of her skirt. A girl's skirt is too short if it is so distracting that the other students or the teacher cannot concentrate in class.

As we get older, we tend to conveniently forget what we were like when we were young. Every one of us wore, or wanted to wear, something that was against our authority figure's rules. Teens are influenced by fads, and the way they dress is an attempt to fit in or illustrate to the world who they think they are. I don't advocate allowing students to wear gang colors or anything that could harm anyone. One of our main goals in a school is to provide a safe learning environment, and we must react swiftly and decisively when it comes to protecting our students. But we also need to remember that the vast majority of the kids in our schools are rather reasonable, good people. Just as it's a huge mistake to punish an entire class for the misdeeds of a few, it's wrong to force all the students to follow rules designed to reign in the few with poor judgment. We have to be open-minded about people who dress and act differently from ourselves. People should be judged by their actions, not their appearances. They are either functioning as a positive force in the community or they're not.

> *Remember that the vast majority of the kids in our schools are rather reasonable, good people.*

Another of my favorite things about teaching is that everything changes at the ring of a bell. A whole new set of students comes in with a variety of social, religious, racial, and political backgrounds. If teachers become bored with their jobs, it may be because they've focused so hard on teaching a subject they've forgotten that they're really teaching students. We're in a people business, and we have to remain flexible to survive. Not too long ago, a student in one of my classes was killed in a car accident. Former students of mine have died before, but never while they were members of my class. The young man died because he and his friend had been drinking. He was by no means a top student; Eddie had been involved in gangs and had just returned from the alternative school because he'd been caught smoking on campus so many times. He had a learning disability and an extremely short fuse. To top it off, he was hyperactive, which had caused some real headaches for many teachers. But in my experience, he was kindhearted, funny, and great with computers. He and I got along because he knew I liked him, and I would not allow him to behave inappropriately in class.

They kept Eddie on a life-support system for two days after the accident. As I was leaving school that Monday, the office secretary called to let me know Eddie had died. I knew the next day would be difficult not only because I felt terrible but because I knew many of his friends would be upset as well. On Tuesday morning, one of our counselors announced over the public-address system that Eddie had died and asked us to think about him during the moment of silence that begins every school day. This brought a few tears to my eyes, but I started to lose it when a senior who had been in a gang with Eddie came into my room, threw his arms around me, and started crying. I took him out into the hall and we both cried a little out there. I calmed him down, sent him back to class, and headed to the front office to wash my face. Halfway there, one of the male teachers asked me to go into the girls' restroom because he could hear screeching and loud noises. I found nine girls, some lying on the floor, crying their eyes out. I sat down and tried to talk to them a bit, but they were extremely upset and more girls were joining them. Finally, I asked them to come sit with me in the cafeteria so we wouldn't block the door. By then, I was surrounded by about 20 girls and boys, most of whom were crying. I sat next to one girl who was almost hysterical; I rubbed her back and let her sit close to me. Just when I had them calmed down, an administrator came by and asked what we were doing. I told her that these students had been friends of Eddie and needed someone to talk to. She said that unfortunately, these things do happen, but it was best just to stay busy and not dwell on them. Then she ordered everyone back to class. I had to physically restrain one girl from attacking her. I told the administrator as calmly as I could that I would sit with these students for a while but that she needed to send a counselor to talk with them. She pressed her lips together and marched off. No one came, even after I sent two other people to ask for help. Finally, I took the group, which had swollen to about 30 students, back to my room. I had a first-period class, I was in the middle of preparing my seniors to write their research papers, and I didn't want to spend my day trying to talk with these kids who weren't even my students. But I also had to be flexible enough to realize that this was an extraordinary situation, and the best lesson I could teach that day was compassion.

Period after period, students filed into my room to sit and cry or mourn. During that day, I was able to talk to gang members and students who were abusing alcohol and drugs about the likely consequences of their choices. The administrators had presented a program at the last teachers' meeting about gangs, and we had discussed ways to keep gangs from polluting our school. But not one administrator came down to my room to talk to these kids. They were there—the gang members—and they were in a vulnerable state. The door was open, and no one came. True, these were some of the most difficult kids in the school. True, they were supposed to be in class, and they were breaking the rules by coming to my room. True, this one incident would probably not change everything, but it could change some things.

> *I love teaching because of the combination of left-brain linear, logical work and right-brain creative, intuitive work.*

We have all heard of the *teachable moment*, that magic time when what you say is exactly what the student needs (and is ready) to hear. It doesn't happen all the time, but as a teacher, you have to be flexible enough to grab it. I love teaching because of the combination of left-brain linear, logical work and right-brain creative, intuitive work. My songwriter friend understands this miracle. Often he'll work on a song for several months, fine-tuning it or even changing it completely. But every once in a while, a song drops into his lap finished, and he has to scramble to get it written down before it goes away. I call this the funnel to heaven, and I believe gifted people can access this. I never enter a classroom without a lesson plan, but teaching is a performance art; if you leave yourself open to that funnel, you can sometimes improvise a metaphor or connection that makes the whole lesson click for the kids. The lights go on and you see the great "Aha!" leap into their eyes. That's what keeps us coming back, year after year.

Sometimes, a lesson I've presented about something as seemingly mundane as writing a business letter can evolve into a life-altering experience. Chuck was a student in senior English who came with a warning sticker practically stamped on his forehead. He was an infamous troublemaker with a volatile temper. Whenever I teach business letters, I point out how powerful they are as problem-solving tools. I show examples of letters that have generated solutions or opportunities for me; I also talk about how a well-written letter can be far more effective than an angry phone call. One day, I was sitting in my room during my planning period and the door slammed open. Chuck burst in, and I could see immediately he was about to explode. He asked me if he could use one of my computers, and I said, "Okay, but don't break it." I could tell he didn't want to talk, so I worked at my desk while he typed away. After much mumbling, he brought a beautifully crafted business letter to my desk for me to read. It turned out he'd been accused of doing something, not because of any proof, but because of his reputation. He asked me to show him how to change the format so he could address the letter to all of the school board members and the superintendent of our district. I was stunned. This was a kid who normally would have slashed the principal's tires or torn down the paper-towel holders in the bathrooms. Now, he was using something I'd taught him to solve a problem in an adult manner. I couldn't have been more proud.

If you keep an open mind and are flexible, you can take advantage of unexpected opportunities to bring a lesson home and really get through to a struggling student. In a senior vocational English class, I worked with a group of self-proclaimed "skater-punks" who were constantly clashing with teachers and administrators about the dress code. Teachers would grab them in the hall and yank up their pants or pull off their wallet chains. The students had very little respect for authority figures, and most were in school only because they'd lose their driver's licenses if they quit. They were a real challenge to teach. I'd been having trouble convincing these boys that what I was teaching could be of use to them; but as luck would have it, the administrators sent out a lengthy memo outlining a new, rather strict dress code and asked all teachers to read it to their classes. This caused general outrage among the students, even those who would never dream of wearing anything out of the ordinary to school because of the dictatorial nature of the mandate. I overheard one of the leaders of the skaters planning some mayhem for after school, so I quietly joined the group and complimented them for playing right into the administrators' hands. They looked at me suspiciously as I told them causing some destruction to the school would be the best way possible for the administrators to justify their strict rules. The administrators could then say, "See, these kids are out of hand, and we have to crack down on them!"

Michael, the leader, asked me if I thought they should just roll over and take it. I told him both solutions he'd suggested—senseless violence or passivity—sounded pretty chicken to me. He bristled all over and asked what I thought they should do. I wanted to know if they were really interested in challenging the dress code or if they just wanted to rage against the machine. I also asked them if they were willing to put in the extra time and attention a real solution would require. They assured me they were serious and tired of being pushed around. So I altered my lesson plans right there and created a unit to show them how to be proactive rather than reactive.

> *Because we work with people, we have to be ready to embrace the unexpected and make it work.*

Talk about student motivation! This group of nine kids who rarely worked in any class became a dynamic organization. They started by interviewing the administrators to get the facts behind the new rules. Then they developed a questionnaire to poll other students and teachers about their opinions about the dress code. Next, the students drafted a report summarizing all of the results and offering suggestions for a compromise. Finally, we invited the principal to class, at which time Michael orally presented their findings. When he left, the principal had a professional-looking, 20-page report and a new vision of these kids. He didn't throw out the new dress code, but he did make modifications. My students were exhilarated by the experience, and all nine went on to graduate.

A flexible, open-minded attitude can be infectious. When I started teaching at this rural Tennessee high school, I was assigned to teach vocational English. The vocational director was an older man, who was also a farmer on the side. He didn't know what to think of this crazy woman from California who spoke and acted so differently from everyone else. He viewed all of us foreigners with suspicion, and although he was nice, he kept me at arm's length. One day, I came to him with a proposal for a project I wanted to try with my students. He hemmed and hawed and didn't know how to respond. Finally I said, "You know, if we combine some Tennessee *know-how* with some California *why not*, we could create the best vocational English program in the state." He loved the idea and helped me get my first computers. Some of my colleagues thought I was a laid-back, west-coast flower child because I did unusual things in my classes and I stood up for the rights of my students. Actually, if they ever had the chance to watch me teach, they'd see that I'm organized to a fault and tolerate very few inappropriate behaviors. I just understand that because we work with people, we have to be ready to embrace the unexpected and make it work. The eighth commandment of good teaching? Thou shalt be open-minded and flexible to be successful.

9

Thou Shalt Not Work in Fear

You train people how to treat you by how you treat yourself.

—Martin Rutte

My entire teaching career has been a series of successes and failures. The successes have given me the confidence and the reputation that have earned me the freedom I enjoy. But my own best teacher has always been failure. A sign that hangs above the computers in my room says, "People who never make mistakes work for people who aren't afraid to." I've made about every mistake in the book, but each one has helped me refine my program, allowing me to rewrite a rule or throw out a lesson and add another. After teaching for six years, I decided to put a couch in my classroom so my students could be comfortable when they were reading. It's a struggle to get some of my students to even open a book; therefore, I'm constantly searching for ways to help them associate reading with pleasure. It seemed like a great idea, but even with the best of intentions, students would nod off with a book on their chests. They would also fight over who got to sit on the couch, and I finally decided the couch was causing more problems than it was worth. I went back to a table and chairs the following year.

You can't expect your first year (or any year) of teaching to be stress free, and you certainly shouldn't give up just because there were problems. You can allow the problems to defeat you or you can analyze what worked, give yourself credit for what went well, and change what didn't. You need to take chances every year because if you try to please everyone, you'll end up pleasing no one, especially yourself.

> Successes have given me the confidence and the reputation that have earned me the freedom I enjoy. But my own best teacher has always been failure.

I've had teachers sit in my class watching every move I make then try to teach exactly as I do. It never works. You have to create your own style, from your own passion, and build enough confidence in it to help you weather the inevitable criticism. There is never a point in time when everyone is thrilled with what you're doing—it's not possible. I used to moan and groan over the one or two students each year who seemed to hate my class. After listening to this for a while, a friend finally asked, "How about the majority who loved what you did?" That really helped me to shift my focus from the failures to the successes. A person who pleases everyone is probably teaching within such safe borders, there is no room for growth.

Watch everyone, learn from everyone, but follow your instincts. When designing my classes, I knew I could never live with total quiet or total chaos, so I found a place somewhere between the two that matches my rhythms. Teachers are often guilty of criticizing a colleague who teaches in a different style just because it's not how they would do it. Schools would be pretty dull places if everyone taught and learned in exactly the same manner. My daughters have two favorite teachers in common. One was a strict disciplinarian who lectured 95% of the time; the other was a child-centered person who encouraged creativity and risk. The girls loved both of them. These teachers had found their own styles, which freed them to communicate their love for their subjects, and that's all that mattered. Leave yourself open to all suggestions, but use your instincts and experiences to filter out the ones that don't work for you.

To be successful as a teacher, you have to understand the balance of power in the system. When I'm teaching my seniors about succeeding in their chosen careers, I ask them to draw a chart showing the balance of power in our school district. I tell them to place the most important people on top and the least important people at the bottom. It amazes me that year after year the kids put the superintendent at the top and the students at the bottom. They're shocked when I tell them that they have it all wrong. They need to turn their charts upside down to view them correctly. The most important people in our school systems are the students and their parents. They pay our salaries through taxes, and we work for them. The seniors love it when I place the teachers right under the students and a few decide to make some personnel changes before the end of the day. One of my favorite responses when students ask, "Why do you make us do so much work?" is "Because that's what you hired me to do. Do you want me to waste your money?" Below the teachers on my version of this chart come the counselors and support personnel. Next are the administrators, and finally, we add the superintendent and school board. You may think I'm being facetious, but think about the logic here. The principal's job is to clear the way for me to teach. He works for me in that he removes anything that keeps me from doing the best job I can. The superintendent works for the principal in the same manner. She provides whatever is required to make the principal successful in his job. This may seem topsy-turvy at first, but without students, we have no jobs. We're the only employees in the world who can have dissatisfied customers and stay in business. The government is continually threatening to distribute vouchers that will make everyone view the balance of power in the schools in a different way. Tenure may soon become a thing of the past.

When you begin teaching in a school, you'd be wise to uncover where the true power lies. Many new teachers live in terror of their principals or supervisors, but administrators are not necessarily the most influential people in a school. During the lesson on the balance of power, I ask my students to name the two people in the school for whom I'll do anything—the two people I most want to keep happy because they can make or break my job. The kids are always surprised when I identify the people I need the most as the bookkeeper and the head maintenance man. I have found these two to be the bottom-line experts on almost every project I've tried to get off the ground. Sometimes, I'll see teachers or administrators treat janitors, maintenance personnel, and secretaries like poor relations; that is a huge mistake. If angered, these people can cause you more trouble than any principal could hope to do.

The head of maintenance for my last school has worked there since it opened. He moves slowly and doesn't say much. He has little formal education, and some teachers treat him as they would a servant when they demand his services. The mistake they make is in underestimating his intelligence and not noticing the twinkle in his eye. I've seen him stand calmly while an irate teacher chewed him out about something broken in her classroom. The teacher usually finishes by saying she wants the problem taken care of *immediately*. Mr. P. just stands there and waits for her to finish. Then he tells her he will file the necessary paperwork right away. First, he'll submit the forms to the secretary, who'll get the principal's approval. Then the forms are sent to the central office, where they are processed and returned to him. He hopes, he tells the teacher, to get the go-ahead before the end of the week. Then he walks off with that twinkle in his eye. The truth is Mr. P. runs the school and can fix anything he chooses when he chooses. The teacher is foolish to fail to recognize how important Mr. P. is and to give him the respect he deserves.

> *The kids are always surprised when I identify the two people I need the most as the bookkeeper and the head maintenance man.*

The best way to survive all of the nonsense and politics occurring in any business is to find your people, do everything you can to keep them happy, and operate through them. One of my best friends in my school is a technology teacher. He and I think very much alike, and we both make it our business to ensure the other's success. My classroom used to be directly above Steve's, and he used that to my advantage. We had a supervisor from the central office who dropped by the schools every so often, not to encourage and support what was going well, but to sniff out what was wrong. Steve and I would amuse ourselves by driving this man crazy. For example, if Steve noticed that the supervisor had entered the building, he'd flip on a rarely used band saw that let everyone in the area know that a negative force was on the loose. We never really had anything to hide, but it was fun.

> *The best way to survive all of the nonsense and politics that occur in any business is to find your people, do everything you can to keep them happy, and operate through them.*

One time this supervisor came to my room to observe me. He was armed with about 20 very detailed forms that, when passed through an elaborate scoring system, would tell him whether I was doing a good job or not. He was a big supporter of the state model for teaching, which specifically timed a teacher as he or she moved through the narrow confines of their idea of the ideal lesson plan. When I saw what he was doing, I told him I was glad that beginning or poor teachers had such a model to help them out, but that he'd be crazy to ask someone like me to alter a program that had proved to be successful. He became rather agitated, but when he added up all the numbers, I was one point away from a perfect score.

You have no idea how angry that made him. I taught in a completely different style from that in which he had been trained, but it still worked.

There will always be people similar to this rigid supervisor in your life, and you have to choose how much control to give them. You already know that I'm not afraid of authority figures, but over the years, I have learned when to shut up. There are things that go on in school every day that could upset me; I've just gotten better at picking and choosing my battles.

This was a hard lesson I learned when I was just starting out. I was hired to teach reading and English at a high school in central California. Being the new kid on the block, I was assigned to a portable classroom. When I went in to set it up, I discovered that I had only half the number of desks I needed. I went to the front office, straightforwardly introduced myself to the vice-principal, and told him I needed 12 desks right away. To my surprise, his face closed up, and he said, "We have many teachers who need many things; I'll put your request on a list, but you may just need to make do." I was stunned and embarrassed because what I wanted seemed so reasonable. As I left his office, it occurred to me that it wasn't my request that was hard to take, it was my manner. I was a young woman with a lot of confidence, but he had perceived me as a pushy female. I waited a few hours, and then I returned to his office. This time I acted contrite and confused and told him I really needed his help because I was so nervous about my first job and could he please help out poor, pathetic me. I had the desks within 30 minutes. I felt horrible that I had played the "helpless female" to get what I wanted, but I also learned that the desks were more important than forcing him to treat me with respect. That would come later.

If someone is doing something to harm a student, physically or emotionally, I fight that battle. If someone is simply being annoying, I just ignore him. Often students come into my class ready to hurt someone because that person had said something they didn't like. My advice is that unless this person is threatening to harm someone, don't pay any attention.

Students find this very difficult to do, so I offer them my favorite trick. When a person is being ridiculous, yelling at me about a problem I don't own, I visualize him or her as a yappy dog. This allows me to listen and nod, but get no more emotionally involved than I would with a terrier at my ankles. It is completely my choice whether I let this person ruin my day.

> *It is completely my choice whether I let this person ruin my day.*

Most of what goes on outside your classroom is not worthy of your attention, but there are fights you can't be afraid to take on. One year, the principal in my school decided to eradicate drugs from the high school by strip-searching selected students. A surprise announcement came over the PA system instructing us to allow no one to leave classrooms until further notice. We were to wait until a messenger came to our doors to escort certain students to the front office where male and female police officers were waiting. I have always abhorred this reactionary method of controlling drug abuse, but I did what I could to calm my students by pointing out that if they were innocent, they had nothing to worry about. I stood out in the hallway watching the administrators pull students out of classes. Suddenly, it dawned on me that the only students taken to the office were the "hoods" or those from poor families. Without exception, all the males had long hair and all of the females were dressed in leather or "biker" clothes. I asked another teacher to watch my class and ran to the office to find the principal. I asked him to tell me what criteria were used to select these students. He told me not to get involved, that he knew who the druggies were, and to go back to class. I pointed out that just because students had long hair or didn't look like his idea of "clean-cut," it didn't automatically mean they were using drugs. I told him if he was really interested in finding the drug abusers, he should pull in a few athletes or some of the rich kids who had the money to spend. He ordered me back to class, and I told him I hoped he would publish the results of this search so we could all see its effectiveness.

Later that day, I was in my room by myself and one of the kids who had been taken to the office came in. Carl was a tough kid from an extremely poor family. In fact, his mother had died and his father bothered to check on his children only every once in a while. Carl had a foul mouth, was overtly racist, and rarely wore clean clothes. He was constantly in fights at school because of his inability to accept any point of view other than his own. I had been trying for months to get him to see how the racist attitude his father had taught him was simply a pathetic attempt to make someone at the bottom rung of society's ladder feel superior to someone else. I'd had little luck, and I sure didn't think the current tension in the room could turn into a teachable moment. He stormed over to me and leaned against the counter where I was working. He avoided my eyes, but I could see he'd been crying. I asked him what had happened, and he almost started crying again. "Ms. Gill, they strip-searched me—they didn't find nothin' because I don't do drugs. I told them that but they didn't care." He slammed his fist against the counter, and I told him how sorry I was. The anger was spilling out of him. "They didn't care who I was; I ain't got the money to dress like no rich kid so they just assumed I was guilty." I told him only foolish or scared people judge others by their appearance. He sputtered, "They just look down on my daddy, but I'll get my daddy to come down here and kill 'em all. They don't know nothing about me!" At this point, I said that he must be feeling the same kind of frustration a black person feels when all anyone can see is the color of his skin. Carl looked at me shocked, and for just a moment, I saw a shift in his eyes, but it was gone as quickly as it appeared. I spent the next 10 minutes trying to calm Carl down, but I know that for just a moment he knew that the stupid way the administrators handled him matched the ignorance he'd shown toward blacks for years. By the way, after humiliating more than 90 students with a strip-search, the administrators found two marijuana seeds in the borrowed jacket of one of the students.

A few years later, a new principal ordered a similar lockdown of the entire school, brought in dogs, and searched the purses, backpacks, and pockets of each of the 1,350 students in our school. This time they confiscated aspirin, Midol, cigarettes, lighters, vitamins, and pocketknives. They found no illegal drugs or weapons. We published the results of the search in the school newspaper.

Yes, for reasons that still elude me, my former principal and the English department chairperson signed me up to teach journalism. I had never taken a journalism class in my life, but I was excited by the challenge. We hadn't had a newspaper in our school for many years, and no one wanted to fool with it. To everyone's amazement, my initial staff of 10 produced a 12-page, tabloid-sized monthly publication that regularly sold out within 20 minutes.

> *When you give in too many times, you may gain job security but lose the integrity that will make you a great teacher.*

During my second year of teaching the journalism class, I was in a meeting where the principal mentioned that he had misinformed the student body about the number of absences they could accrue before automatically failing a class. At that time, he admitted he was in violation of school-board policy, but to avoid total confusion, he wasn't going to revise his policy until the end of the school year. I saw his point in that it would require a great deal of expense and paperwork to fix the problem midstream, so I didn't say anything. About a month later, three of my journalism students came to me with the news that two seniors had dropped out of school because of the misinformation. I immediately went to my principal and told him we would be glad to print a clarification in the next issue of the school newspaper to avoid any further confusion. He ordered me to leave the matter alone. I knew he was afraid of losing his job over the issue, but I tried to make him understand that this wrong information was actually causing harm to the students. He told me the newspaper was his and he had every right to censor what we printed. I told him that he was welcome to assign someone else to produce a public relations sheet for his administration, but I was assigned to help publish a student newspaper. After a heated debate, I recognized he would continue to place his best interests over the students', so I got up to leave. When I reached the door, he asked me if I understood what he expected me to do. I turned around and told him he could always count on me to protect the students, something I consider to be our first responsibility as teachers. I knew what was at stake, but we printed the correct information, and the principal never said another word to me about it.

A friend of mine wrote a song in which she described a poet as a "boat rocker in a deep river," and I identify with that image. At this point in my life, it would be so much easier to stay in my room and wait for retirement. I've noticed that I don't feel the same fire for the problems that surface year after year—the dress code, the complicated record-keeping systems, the scrambling for power. I have a wonderful job and could easily sail through the next few years. But there is always the student who has been denied rights or the good teacher who is ready to quit because of feeling overwhelmed by the system. I've just learned to be a little better at compromise, and I try more often to make sure I have all the facts before I jump in. I've found a few kindred spirits who encourage me but aren't afraid to tell me when I'm wrong, and I try to see things from other points of view. New teachers are often afraid to stand up for themselves, their fellow teachers, or their students until they have tenure. However, when you give in too many times, you may gain job security but lose the integrity that will make you a great teacher. It's a delicate balance, and the mentors you choose can help you stay on track. The ninth commandment of good teaching? Thou shalt not work in fear; just be sure you're right and that the battle is worth fighting.

10

Thou Shalt Raise Your Expectations

By any means necessary. . . .

—Malcolm X

O ne of the biggest mistakes we can make as educators is to view students as empty vessels just waiting for us to remove their lids and pour in the knowledge. As Jake Barnes says to Lady Brett Ashley in *The Sun Also Rises,* "Wouldn't it be pretty to think so?" But the reality is that the students come to us with all levels of skills, experiences, and expectations. Our challenge is to move them all forward, and this can be an overwhelming task.

I believe in no-excuses teaching. It may be true that kids these days have become increasingly difficult to teach. The majority come from broken homes, some live in nightmarish conditions, and others view school as a total waste of time. Either because of the changes in the evaluation system or because of the unstable conditions in which they live, I find

I'm working with more and more students with learning disabilities. I can think of a million reasons to believe these kids are not teachable, but I refuse to do that. This is one area in which I choose to work in ignorance.

When I first started teaching in a small-town high school, a colleague who had lived in the community all her life asked to see my roll sheets. She knew I was new to the area, and she wanted to help me out. She proceeded to call out the names on my roster, letting me know this student was from a good family, that one was bad news, this kid was the mayor's son, that one's daddy was in jail. I was horrified and purposely ignored what she was saying. When the students enter my room at the first of the year, they are all the same to me. I pay no attention to what another teacher has to say about a student's potential. I rely on the counseling office to let me know about any medical or emotional problems that may affect the students' performances, but other than that, I want to gather my own impressions.

One of the ways I know teachers are headed for burnout is when they begin to offer more and more excuses as to why their students can't be taught. There's always a reason: overcrowded classes, not enough technology, indifferent parents, a test-run curriculum, lack of funds, hostile students, and so on. When your conversation starts sounding similar to this, you need to clearly separate the things you can do something about from the things beyond your control. Teachers rarely accept a student's excuse for being tardy or not turning in homework. They point out that life is not fair and there are no excuses on the job. We teachers are on the job, life is not fair, and we shouldn't make excuses either; we need to fix what we can and get a little more clever about the rest.

> *There are three kinds of people: those who make things happen, those who watch things happen, and those who say, "What happened?"*

One year, the counseling office put 29 students in my remedial reading lab. I didn't find out until the day before school started. I told the counselors that they had to remove

14 students because the reading lab was designed for a maximum of 15. They said it was a computer mix-up, but the students were already scheduled in and they'd try to fix it for next semester. I told them they had to make a decision. Did they want me to teach these students to read, or did they want to use me for crowd control? It was up to them. They told me many teachers had overcrowded classes that year and asked me if I thought I was special. I said that my students certainly are. Luckily, they agreed to put in the extra time to fix the error. I'm not sure what I would have done if they hadn't made the change. I do know that I would not have passively accepted my fate or spent the year complaining to my colleagues. I would have found a way.

> *I believe the worst thing you can do to students is to feel sorry for them. There are no remedial jobs in real life.*

Another one of the signs in my room says, "There are three kinds of people: those who make things happen, those who watch things happen, and those who say, 'What happened?'" I don't believe in being a squeaky wheel just to see what kind of noise I can make, but I do believe in setting up the best learning atmosphere possible and then doing whatever is necessary to protect it. I begin each class expecting all my students to succeed, and I do everything in my power to make sure they do—whatever it takes.

In the same manner, I expect a lot out of my students because I believe kids either live up or down to my expectations. I firmly believe a teacher can maintain high standards and still have a very small percentage of failures. I also believe the worst thing you can do to students is to feel sorry for them. There are no remedial jobs in real life. When the kids face the world of work, no one will let them do less than what is required because of pity. There have been times when other people thought I was being mean to certain students by holding them to the same standards as the rest of the class. Robert, a student with Down syndrome, was placed in my reading lab because he needed to learn to socialize outside his special education class. He was 16 years old and few teachers had required him to do much because he had problems controlling his emotions. Usually, they just let Robert sit in the back of the class and do whatever kept him quiet. When I agreed to let him into my reading class, I told his parents I would expect him to work just like my other students. They readily agreed, and I spent some extra time teaching Robert to use the computers and operate in the groups of my class. One day, an administrator asked me to step outside of my classroom for a moment to ask me a question; I told Robert's group I'd be working with them next and to be ready as soon as I got back. When I returned, Robert was on the floor crying and several students were standing helplessly around him. They told me he'd become upset over something and wouldn't get up. I walked over to him, told him it was time to get to work, and asked that as long as he was down there, would he mind getting that piece of paper behind that counter? I hadn't been able to reach it myself. Several students looked at me, horrified I had shown so little concern for the emotional state of this special child. Robert glanced up at me, gave a couple more sobs, but quickly retrieved the paper and joined his group at my table. As the semester progressed, he learned to type and mail business letters and work cooperatively in a group. He, his parents, and I were delighted with his success.

Another student who pulled at my heart was in my senior English class. Linda was a little out of her league, but did not want to take a remedial English class. She struggled through most of her assignments but was willing to correct what was wrong. Midway through the year, she woke up one morning to find her mother dead on the sofa. Her father wasn't in the picture, and she had one married brother who was not much support. As you can imagine, she missed a number of school days and was overwhelmed when she returned. I did everything in my power to help her catch up, but she continued to miss days because of depression or illness. When I averaged the final grades for her class, we discovered that she had not passed. She burst into tears and begged me to change her grade as many of her other teachers had done. Knowing she planned to work as a secretary when she graduated from high school, I told her that her writing skills were not even close to what they needed to be. She begged me to think of a way for her to do extra credit work, and I promised I would. When she came to see me the next day, I had a packet of work designed to remediate what she had failed and improve her writing abilities. I told her that most of it needed to be typed and it had to be completed within two weeks. I offered to stay after school every day to help her. Her heart sank when she saw the amount of work, but she took it with her. Later in the day, another teacher told me he'd seen Linda crying in the cafeteria because she had so much to do. I know he thought I was torturing this child who had suffered so much already, but I tried to explain that by just handing her a grade she didn't deserve, I'd be doing her a real disservice. Luckily, Linda rose to the challenge and completed all the necessary work to pass with a D–. I attended graduation mostly for her, and even though it had been a struggle, she was able to proudly claim the diploma she had earned.

You need to constantly raise your expectations for yourself.

I also believe you need to constantly raise your expectations for yourself. After years of refining, I'm finally satisfied with the design of my regular English class, but I would never dream of resting there. Just as my students change every year, what is required of them in the real world changes. I have to stay up to date with materials and technology or I'll be holding my students back. When I was student teaching, I worked under a teacher who was very generous with his materials. I was flipping through a stack of his files and was dismayed to find the masters to several handouts he reprinted over and over. This teacher had been giving his students the exact same worksheets for 20 years. I'm sure some of it was useful, worthy information, but I would challenge his method for two reasons. One, the sheer volume of facts available to students increases exponentially every year, and what is required of them on the job is in a constant state of flux. Two, one of the quickest roads to burnout is to teach the same thing year after year in the same way. I was terrified when I was assigned to teach the journalism class because it definitely moved me out of my area of expertise. In retrospect, it revitalized me. The same thing happened every time I moved to a new school. The easy road is to stay with the familiar. It's much more difficult to become a learner again and scramble to stay ahead of the students, but our energy and enthusiasm will be contagious.

During the first faculty meeting, administrators usually distribute the list of the teachers to be evaluated that year. This is often greeted with moans and groans as the teachers anticipate the extra work required. To be honest, I'm not crazy about someone coming into my class to tell me what I'm doing wrong. However, I have never failed to learn something from an evaluation. Sometimes, it reinforces my belief in the way I teach. Other times, it makes me question or defend what I'm doing. In either case, it helps me to become a better teacher. I'm not so foolish as to passively accept every suggestion the evaluator may make, but I'm also not so foolish as to think that what I do is perfect and cannot be improved. Even when I think a criticism is dead wrong, it makes me go back and look at my lesson to see why the observer would interpret it incorrectly. If I think my evaluator just missed the point of what I did, I ignore the critique. If something can be improved, I incorporate the suggestions into my classroom routine.

In the long run, my most useful evaluators are my students. Who better knows the quality of my work? Attached to the final exam for each of my classes is an evaluation sheet. I ask the students to specifically describe the activities we did that were the most and the least useful to them. I also want to know why. I tell them before I hand out the exam that I tear the evaluation sheet off before I grade their tests, and I won't look at it until the final grades are on their report cards. I want them to give me honest feedback to help me improve my classes, and buttering me up or putting me down does not affect their grades in any way. I pay close attention to what my students tell me. Sometimes, I'm baffled that a unit I was particularly proud of was more or less meaningless to them. Then again, they'll surprise me by wanting more of the repetitive work I thought they'd find boring, such as grammar and spelling exercises. Whenever I run into former graduates, I ask them to tell me about the things we did in class that turned out to be useful to them later on. I never take a negative evaluation personally; that would be similar to students who throw fits because they receive an F on a test. An evaluation is nothing more than useful information about someone else's perception of what I'm doing. The only people who need to fear evaluations are those who refuse to grow.

In the long run, my most useful evaluators are my students. Who better knows the quality of my work?

A friend of mine has a philosophy that used to drive me nuts, but I've now come to embrace it. He often says, "Just because something is impossible is not a good enough reason to not try." Despite its awkward wording, it holds much truth. We live in the United States, one of the few countries in the world that attempts to educate its entire populace. As teachers, we face an impossible job. We are asked to accept every product, no matter how flawed and get it ready to work. We are asked to be calm, intelligent, loving role models day after day, year after year. We are asked to work through the layers of disuse to find the spark that ignites a student to discover the meaning of his or her life. We are asked to accept that we will never be paid what we're worth and that many of the miracles we perform will go unappreciated. But as I said earlier, if it were easy, anyone could do it. As a teacher, you are part of an elite group of people who can improve the lives of other human beings. The tenth commandment of good teaching? Thou shalt raise your expectations for yourself and your students.

11

Thou Shalt Keep Things in Perspective

People only see what they are prepared to see.

—Ralph Waldo Emerson

The last year of the century ended like the opening lines of *A Tale of Two Cities;* it was truly the best and the worst of times for me. By October 1999, I was at the top of my game as a teacher. I had received a wall full of awards from my school district and various organizations and had been selected as one of six finalists for Tennessee's State Teacher of the Year. My book sales and seminars were going well, and I had a number of articles published in professional journals. I loved my job, and because of my history there, I could get almost anything I wanted done just by making a few phone calls. I had an excellent relationship with my new principal, and many of my coworkers thought of me as a good source of information and guidance. I continued to hear from former students who told me my class was one of their favorites or that something I said had changed the direction of their lives. My daughters all lived nearby and were self-supporting, even though two were still in college. Life was good. But by June 2000, my 25-year marriage had ended, I had sold my house, quit my job, and was sitting in a Ryder truck with my brother and all of my worldly goods. I was headed back to California, 2,000 miles away from my children and the life I'd lived for 17 years.

During the last year I lived in Tennessee, I felt like two of the biggest sources of comfort in my life had turned on me— my husband and my students. How could this have happened after all I'd given to them? I covered myself in a cloak of self-pity and railed against such an unfair universe. My marriage was crumbling because of circumstances beyond my control, and every day in second period, I had to face the worst class of my teaching career. The ingrates! I wanted an audit from the cosmic forces—the books weren't balancing and I deserved better than this! For the first time in my life, I began viewing myself as a victim.

I had never written a book about marriage, but I had written one about teaching. The irony did not escape me as I watched a small group of students take control of my class and spin me around like a novice. I knew I was in trouble when I showed the list of students to a colleague and she burst out laughing. "Who did you make mad?" she chuckled. "It looks like they've put every behavior problem in the twelfth grade together in one class." That wasn't far from the truth; I recognized several of the students' names because they were legends—students who could bring teachers to tears, students whose parents had given several administrators ulcers, and students who feared neither failure nor expulsion because they had been diagnosed as having specific learning disabilities or behavior disorders and felt they could not be held accountable for their actions. These students were not at all impressed by me or the honor of being in my class.

I spent what seemed to be too much time walking around feeling sorry for myself. There were days when I was filled with anger over these people who were making my life so miserable. One afternoon, I was walking into an optometrist's office when I stepped aside for a man and a woman who were leaving the building. The husband held the door wide for his wife, and I couldn't help but notice that both of her arms had been amputated below the elbows. I felt a little flustered, but she smiled graciously and she and her husband continued joking about the new frames he had chosen. He gallantly guided her into their car, giving her a kiss on the cheek before he shut the door. That tiny moment had a huge impact on my life. As I waited for my appointment, I looked in the mirror that lined the walls of the office and said to myself, "You have no problems." Driving home that evening, I realized that even though I was dealing with some stressful circumstances, I'd allowed myself to fall into the trap of blaming my misery on external circumstances against which I was helpless.

Several years ago, I wrote a letter to a friend of one of my daughters who was having a difficult time. I told him we view life through a prism. Tilted one way, the lines can seem blurred and distorted, but a slight shift towards the light creates a glorious cascade of colors. After seeing the woman at the eye doctor, I consciously shifted my perspective from obsessing over my weaknesses to focusing on my strengths. Even though I mourned the end of my marriage, I had been married to a musician for 25 years (which is a miracle in itself), and we had raised three remarkable young women who continue to be a source of great pleasure. And yes, I was dealing with an unusually difficult group of students, but what a wonderful opportunity to practice what I'd been preaching all these years.

The first thing I did was to stop concentrating on what my students were doing wrong and figure out which of the commandments of good teaching I was breaking. I realized that my two biggest errors were taking my students' inappropriate behaviors personally and not asking for help. The kids didn't know me well enough to hate me, but they had learned to hate authority figures and that was how they saw me. I looked up each of their schedules and talked to their other teachers to find out a little more about their lives outside of my class-room. The vocational teachers and coaches were especially helpful because they knew so much about the students' motivations and their families. Then, I made it a point to hang around the cafeteria and in the hallways between classes to talk to the kids informally and find out who their friends were. Instead of seeing the class as one big problem to solve, I looked at them as individuals I needed to get to know. I turned around my relationship with two of the boys because they were good friends with some of my former students. I walked up to the group of them between classes one day and said in mock anger to one of the boys who had loved my class, "Hey, why are you letting Jimmy treat me so badly?" Everyone burst out laughing, and we bantered back and forth about Jimmy's behavior, with Jimmy trying to defend himself and his friends howling over his protests of innocence. This accomplished two things: First, it allowed me to let Jimmy know about the things that were bothering me in an atmosphere of fun; second, it helped Jimmy see me as a person his friends liked.

I worked through the class, finding allies wherever I could, and used my instincts about which approach would be most productive. I'd join some of the students in the cafeteria or library and ask their advice about ways to improve the atmosphere in our class. Another boy did a complete turnaround after I caught his girlfriend and him in an embrace in a back hallway. They expected me to take them to the office, but instead, I asked the girlfriend in all earnestness how come Tony was so sweet with her but so sour with me. Tony blushed, but his girlfriend and I had a great talk, and she made it a point to stop by my class regularly to ask if his behavior had improved. It had—she was quite a motivator. A few of the kids were more difficult, and I had to make behavior contracts with their parents and the counselor, but all in all, the atmosphere of the class improved. I hadn't changed the students; I had changed the way I responded to the students.

> *I hadn't changed the students; I had changed the way I responded to the students.*

Because of my divorce, I had to sell my house and move. My niece was teaching at a small school in California and told me about a job opening there that sounded too good to be true. At first, I dismissed the idea—how could I abandon my children and the career I had worked so hard to build? The idea of moving so far away to rebuild my life seemed selfish; this was not the way I'd pictured my life going. Then, one morning I turned on my computer and a quote by Joseph Campbell popped onto the screen: "We must be willing to let go of the life we have planned, so as to have the life that is waiting for us." Instead of seeing myself as shut out of my old life, I started thinking of myself as setting out on another adventure. Recently, one of my daughters won a scholarship that allowed her to go to Japan for an extended period to study ceramics. We were all thrilled she had such an opportunity. We knew we wouldn't see her for a long time, but none of us ever thought of asking her not to go. My daughters have each let me know in no uncertain terms how proud they are of me for having the courage to embrace the life that's waiting for me.

As I write, everything about my life has changed. I've had the pain and the pleasure of feeling like a new teacher as I became acclimated to my new job. In a short time, I went from being the lady with all the answers to feeling clueless about what I was doing, but the scrambling started a flood of ideas for the new subjects I was teaching. My daughters are two time zones away, but we communicate more than we did when we lived only a few miles apart, only now it is through e-mail and phone calls. Looking back now on the changes in my life, I'm filled with gratitude for my past and excited about the future. Special education students know the difference between a handicap and a challenge. Words and attitudes are incredibly powerful, so we have to be careful to choose the ones that give us the most strength. The eleventh commandment of good teaching? When faced with challenges, thou shalt keep things in perspective. The prism is in our hands.

Epilogue

. . . But they are useless. They can only give you answers.

—Pablo Picasso, about computers

Lately, I've been thinking about Plato's Academy and Stanford University's Wallenberg Hall, trying to figure out how to combine the two. My vision is of Socrates seated in the Plaka surrounded by his students. He poses questions, and with every response, he asks another question. When he pushes his students to the point where they develop a hypothesis, he takes them to a "breakout" classroom with flexible furniture and wireless-Internet access. Students who are searching for similar answers form small groups to work out their ideas on huddleboards. Their notes are converted into digital images using the overhead CopyCam, and they combine their work with other students' ideas to generate a central argument to be proved or disproved. As they research, each on his or her own laptop, they tap into Polycom Internet provider-(IP) based–videoconferencing units to seek primary source information from an oracle at Delphi or Silicon Valley, whichever proves more useful. Toward the end of the period, their teacher calls them together to discuss their findings. They quickly stow their laptops, collapse the tables and chairs, and clear the center of the room to again create a circle at the feet of Socrates, who listens, then asks more questions.

I've accepted a job as a consultant for a small public-school system in central California to help start-up a K–12 charter school. In truth, after so many years of teaching, I had planned on doing something completely different, but the assistant superintendent in charge of the project exudes so much enthusiasm, vision, and idealism that I signed on before I realized the scope of the challenge. I was attracted to the charter's mission statement that included the phrases "real-world applications" and "life-long learners." It was also clear that the people who developed the charter wanted to create small learning communities that were open to educating students in a different way. I even agreed to teach one ninth-grade English class to earn some credibility with the rest of the staff.

My new school is full of energetic and intelligent young teachers fresh from the universities. I've always considered myself to be "techno-friendly"; computers have long been essential to the structure of my class; however, these young teachers make me feel woefully behind the times. Much to my students' amusement, I'm learning to use a digital visual presenter—an updated version of the overhead projector that uses a camera so pages from books and student essays can be easily enlarged for the entire class to view. The science class will soon install a Smart Board that revamps the old-fashioned chalkboard into a touch computer screen. These new teachers are masters of the PowerPoint presentation and have the ability to turn a laptop into a theater system that adds a feast of sights, sounds, and flexibility to the lesson they're presenting. I'm dazzled by the technology, but I feel uneasy at the same time.

As teachers, it's our job to engage our students, and programs like PowerPoint can help us do that. Sounds and images on a big screen are certainly flashier than marks on a whiteboard, and it's easier for the kids in the back to see. I have had the pleasure of observing an English teacher introduce *The Odyssey* using images, maps, and music that had the students panting to open the text. I've also sat through lectures where teachers do nothing more than flash a copy of a worksheet on the screen, and the students are expected to copy down the information in their notes. If the kids are lucky, the teacher will have added some clip art of some sort, but it would be far less tedious if the teacher simply gave everyone a copy of the notes so they wouldn't be writing when the teacher was talking. A couple of years ago, I searched for some type of software that would motivate my students who struggle with grammar and punctuation to spend time on a computer practicing those skills. I envisioned a video game, but most of what I found was nothing more than digital worksheets, which isn't much of an improvement over what language arts teachers have been using for generations. Just because the words are on a screen doesn't make the task more engaging.

Another concern is that some teachers spend so much time preparing and troubleshooting the technology that they have scant time left for the basics: inspiration, discussion, and timely assessment of student work. I have sat through far too many inservice sessions designed to acquaint teachers with programs and online services where a shocking amount of time was wasted on just trying to make the technology work. In fact, I recently decided that if I taught a class for beginning teachers, I'd have each of my students prepare a presentation for the following week. My guess is that most would enter the room with a PowerPoint presentation on their laptops. When the student-teacher faced the room to begin the lesson, I would say, "Now, pretend that your computer has a virus and will not work. All that is available to you is that whiteboard and some markers—present your lesson anyway." They should be able to do that effectively. Again, the technology certainly enhances the lesson, but what it really comes down to is a knowledgeable teacher with the experience to engage students with little more than enthusiasm, solid communication skills, and a deep understanding of the subject matter.

I've also talked to a few teachers who are no longer allowing their students to present their research in a format like PowerPoint or video because often the students focus on the cool special effects and give little attention to the quality and analysis of the information. Last year, professors in top universities, such as Harvard, Columbia, and Yale, banned laptops in the classroom or installed "kill switches" that allow the instructor to turn off the wireless internet network during lectures. One professor said that having the students look at him instead of their screens was like renewing an acquaintance with an old friend. I know exactly what he means. I try to create a casual, friendly environment in my classroom, but my students know that when I'm talking, they have to look my way—like flowers following the sun. I need to see their eyes to know whether or not what I'm saying is making sense. I will loop around a key point, coming at it from several ways, until I see true engagement in every face.

Having said all of this, I would not want to teach without a bank of computers lining the walls of my classroom. They allow me to work with the students individually and in small groups. The computers provide portals for my students to find information from all over the world in a fraction of the time it took me as a kid when all I had were a few sets of out-of-date encyclopedias and the limited number of books in my school's library. Our job as teachers is to create opportunities for students to evaluate and use the products of their research in a meaningful way.

Recently, I was visiting a home where the children were watching a program called "Are You Smarter Than a Fifth Grader?" At one point the adults were called into the room to see if we could answer the $100,000 question: How many feet in a furlong? Whenever I'm in a situation like this—trying to pull trivia out of the air—I'm aware of the alarming number of random facts that are spinning around in my head—evidently this one came and went in the fifth grade. All of the grownups had advanced degrees, but much to the delight of the children, the only person who knew the answer was the 10-year-old on TV. Appearing more like a sore loser than I meant to, I asked the kids if any of them could tell me why it would be useful to know that 660 feet equal a furlong. They all just stared, then one of the girls dashed out of the room and returned with a laptop. Within minutes the children proudly shared the fact that many thoroughbred horse races are measured in furlongs. I applauded their ingenuity, but I was delighted when one of the boys said, "Yeah, but so what?" I told him he was on his way to becoming an educated person—it's all about the "so what?"

We can Google something in a snap, but the challenge is to figure out what to do with all of the information so that we can generate an idea or a compelling connection, which is the goal of research. We teach elementary-school children how to create reports because that gives them practice in reading and writing, but simple regurgitation will not serve the students' needs for long, and it certainly won't help them succeed at the college level or in building a career. They need to learn to synthesize information and develop opinions. In my mind, it's a misuse of the technology to give the students a list of facts to locate, as if finding the right answer was the challenge. As every good English teacher knows, it's not enough for students to look up words in the dictionary and copy down their definitions. They need to play with the connotations of those words before the activity becomes useful.

Because my students have become savvy about accessing online services that offer summaries of great works of literature or prewritten essays that require nothing more than cutting and pasting, I have taken a great deal of pleasure in coming up with assignments that are impossible to find prepackaged on the Internet. I learned this technique from a master teacher whose English final exam required his students to locate a common thread that ran through the texts of disparate works of literature, such as *Hamlet, Winter's Tale, Dreaming in Cuban,* and *The Great Gatsby.* A clever student, with the guidance of the instructor, will grab one of the great themes that run through all of the books, such as "Dreams versus Delusions" or "Does the past determine the future?" and use the Internet to locate definitions and examples. However, the final result will be the student's own—it's highly unlikely that he or she will ever find a paper for sale on any Web site that uses all four of those great works. The key for us as teachers is to show our students how to locate the information efficiently, how to determine the quality of the source, and how to use the research to create connections that will produce original writing.

Sometimes, when I encourage teachers to take the time to identify the *big questions* that will drive their curriculum, they look a little annoyed. They want lesson plans, rubrics, and activity packets. I try to help them realize that plans and activities will naturally occur as the students struggle to figure out the answer to "Why were you put on this Earth?" If asked, they might hypothesize that we're meant to live productive lives, to honor our country and our families, and to do good work. How do we do that? We need to learn how to produce food and protect our environment (science), build shelters (math, art), communicate with one another (reading, writing, speaking), live in peace with our neighbors (foreign languages, social studies), and seek inspiration (art, religion, philosophy, literature, history). Sounds like a typical high school curriculum to me.

As teachers, we cannot ignore the technology—this is a disservice to our students because they will be expected to have mastered these basic tools when they enter college and the workplace. On the other hand, we cannot allow our students to be inundated with data but possess little real information. When you ask kids and adults to talk about their all-time favorite class, the majority of the time they'll describe a teacher; you'd have to probe to get them to mention the technology they used in the class. And when that defiant girl in the back row with the heavy black eyeliner and white lipstick raised her hand to ask, "Why do we have to learn this stuff?" that master teacher might have smiled and answered, "I'm so glad you asked—let me tell you."

References

Berne, E. (1961). *Transactional analysis in psychotherapy: A systematic individual and social psychiatry.* New York: Grove Press.

Berne, E. (1996). *Games people play: The basic handbook of transactional analysis.* New York: Random House.

Ernst, K. (1974). *Games students play (and what to do about them).* Millbrae, CA: Celestial Arts.

Wiggins, G., & McTighe, J. (2005). *Understanding by design.* Alexandria, VA: Association for Supervision and Curriculum Development.

Suggested Reading

Bloom, H. (2000). *How to read and why.* New York: Scribner.

Foster, T. (2003). *How to read literature like a professor.* New York: HarperCollins.

Harris, T. A. (2004). *I'm ok, you're ok.* New York: HarperCollins.

Kozol, J. (1985). *Death at an early age.* New York: Penguin Books.

Kozol, J. (2008). *Letters to a young teacher.* New York: Three Rivers Press.

Macrorie, K. (1985). *Telling writing.* Portsmouth, NH: Heinemann.

Macrorie, K. (1970). *Uptaught.* New York: Hayden Book.

Ward, C. (2006). *How writers grow: A guide for middle school teachers.* Portsmouth, NH: Heinemann.

Williams, D. (1992). *Sin boldly: Dr. Dave's guide to writing the college paper.* New York: Perseus Books Group.

Index

CORWIN
A SAGE Company

The Corwin logo—a raven striding across an open book—represents the union of courage and learning. Corwin is committed to improving education for all learners by publishing books and other professional development resources for those serving the field of PreK–12 education. By providing practical, hands-on materials, Corwin continues to carry out the promise of its motto: **"Helping Educators Do Their Work Better."**